Dedicated to my children, Myles & Charlotte,
who inspire me to be a better human every day.

To our global community of parenting coaches who
inspire me to be a better leader every day.

To my mom for believing in me first. And to Steve, for
continuing to believe in me, even when I waiver.

The Pale Blue Dot

Pale Blue Dot is a famous photograph of planet Earth taken on February 14, 1990, by the Voyager 1 space probe from a record distance of about 6 billion kilometers (3.7 billion miles).

Look again at that dot. That's here. That's home. That's us. On it, everyone you love, everyone you know, everyone you ever heard of, every human being who ever was, lived out their lives. The aggregate of our joy and suffering, thousands of confident religions, ideologies, and economic doctrines, every hunter and forager, every hero and coward, every creator and destroyer of civilization, every king and peasant, every young couple in love, every mother and father, hopeful child, inventor and explorer, every teacher of morals, every corrupt politician, every "superstar," every "supreme leader," every saint and sinner in the history of our species lived there—on a mote of dust suspended in a sunbeam.

The Earth is a very small stage in a vast cosmic arena. Think of the rivers of blood spilled by all those generals and emperors so that, in glory and triumph, they could become the momentary masters of a fraction of a dot. Think of the endless cruelties visited by the inhabitants of one corner of this pixel on the scarcely distinguishable inhabitants of some other corner, how frequent their misunderstandings, how eager they are to kill one another, how fervent their hatreds.

Our posturings, our imagined self-importance, the delusion that we have some privileged position in the Universe, are challenged by this point of pale light. Our planet is a lonely speck in the great enveloping cosmic dark. In our obscurity, in all this vastness, there is no hint that help will come from elsewhere to save us from ourselves.

The Earth is the only world known so far to harbor life. There is nowhere else, at least in the near future, to which our species could migrate. Visit, yes. Settle, not yet. Like it or not, for the moment the Earth is where we make our stand.

—Carl Sagan, Pale Blue Dot, 1994

The Peaceful Parenting (R)evolution

Changing the World
by Changing How We Parent

Kiva Schuler
& The Coaches of The Jai Institute for Parenting

SEACOAST
PRESS

Published by SEACOAST PRESS
1 New Hampshire Ave | Suite 125 | Portsmouth, NH 03801 | USA
603-546-2812 | https://www.seacoastpress.com/

Printed in the United States of America
ISBN-13: 978-1-958729-97-7

A dream you dream alone is only a dream.
A dream you dream together is reality.
—Yoko Ono

CONTENTS

INTRODUCTION

I wasn't going to write this book. I was going to write a different book.

I was selected to attend a writing retreat with Jack Canfield, author of Chicken Soup for the soul.

After I presented my idea about a book on failure, he said, "Kiva, I have to ask: Why aren't you writing a book about parenting?" "Oh, dear," I said. "Because it scares me. I don't consider myself a parenting expert. The very idea of claiming anything of the sort gives me a knot in my stomach." I felt *really* uncomfortable.

"Ummm," Jack pressed harder. "Aren't you the founder of a parenting institute?"

"Well… yeah. But I'm not *the expert!* I'm *just* the founder. The people I hire and train are the experts."

"Besides, there are already so many books on parenting."

"And what do I have to say that hasn't already been said."

"And, oh… how could I possibly take into account all of the diversity, perspectives and experiences that parents face?"

"O.K." He made some notes on his paper. I had flashbacks of presenting my idea for my final project to my very intimidating college advisor. More knots.

"Here's the deal," he said. "You are writing a book on parenting. I want to read your book on parenting. If I want to read your book on parenting, I'm guessing other people do too."

"Send it to me when it's done."

Gulp.

I lay in bed that night, tossing and turning. One of the things I've learned along the way of building the most extensive parent coach training program in the world is that the things that make me the most uncomfortable are the most important.

So, I was going to write this book. But how? I am deeply sensitive to the myriad of challenges, experiences and circumstances that families and children face. I cringe at the idea of making any claim that there are simple frameworks or strategies that make parenting "easy peasy," and therefore create *more* shame when the "easy peasy" strategies don't work in a given family.

Parenting is profound. And profound things are complex. Humans are complex.

At 2 a.m., inspiration jolted me from my bed.

I wouldn't write this book alone. I'd invite a diverse group of our coaches to join me in sharing their stories, insights, and expertise. While I am writing these words, this book is a collaboration of voices. Let me introduce you to your guides as you begin this journey:

Daisy Umenyiora lives in Nigeria. Her gentle soul and passion for bringing more empathy and care to her community, where she essentially became a mother to her siblings at nine, empowers her own children to lead with emotional intelligence.

From suburban Connecticut, Jenny Warner brings decades of human resources experience to her work as a parenting coach, helping families stuck in an achievement cycle create authentic connections and find joy and purpose.

Ashley Kumar, in Toronto, Canada, was adopted into a traditional Indian family, where hierarchical structures of obligation and respect nearly drove her to suicide as a teenager. She now lives in Canada, empowering others through her work as a parenting coach.

Katie Owens is a former therapist who worked with teenagers struggling with gender identity and queerness. She exudes wisdom as she helps families face some of the most challenging experiences parenting can bring to bear, from substance abuse to suicide.

Richard Dixson, from Kansas City, Kansas, is a Black father. He watched his father beat his mother with a shovel when he was a boy. He was determined to be the one to break the generational cycles of violence in his family and now helps other fathers do this through his ministry and work as a parenting coach.

Lina Lie is of Singaporean Chinese descent and struggles with the pressures of her culture to raise children who are a testament to the worthiness of their parents. But she is forging her own path and inspires with her vulnerability and courage to stray from cultural norms.

Christine Irvine is the mother of an autistic daughter and nearly lost connection with her children because she didn't have the tools to meet them in their neurodiversity. She is a powerful model of our premise that everything changes for their children when parents learn the tools of Peaceful Parenting.

Allyn Miller is a former educator, passionate about children and their development. So imagine her surprise when she had her own children and felt unequipped to parent them the way she wanted to! Allyn is a well of knowledge when it comes to the research that supports our methodology.

For six months, I had the pleasure of meeting with this incredible group of parenting coaches weekly. We laughed, cried and shared the stories woven through this book. I also must acknowledge the contribution of Rebecca Lyddon, our Director of Education here at The Jai Institute for Parenting. As the creator of our curriculum, her wisdom sings through these pages.

As I wrote these pages, I experienced a profound realization of my own. I remember one day, after a long writing session, thinking, "thank goodness I am writing this book." Sharing my own stories of being parented and parenting has been deeply healing. And, blushingly, I guess I had more to say than I was giving myself credit for when I said to Jack, "I am *just* the founder."

This work is my soul-work. I am here on this planet to change how parents parent. It has been my calling since I was a child. So thank you, Jack Canfield, for your invitation to own it. I hope that this inspires you to examine your "justs" too!

As you dive into these pages, Richard invites you to have courage as you consider taking this first big step, whether it's awakening a new way of thinking or just processing a different definition of what parenting success looks like for YOU and YOUR FAMILY.

Parenting is not prescriptive. It is a living, breathing dance of meeting the moment with presence and commitment.

❈

As parenting coaches, collectively working with hundreds of families, we hear challenges that seem fairly universal…

- They want to stop yelling at their kids, and they want their kids to listen.
- They are going crazy because their kids won't stop bickering with each other.
- They have older kids demonstrating high-risk behaviors or having a mental health crisis. They are scared.
- They have kids who are underperforming, and they don't know how to motivate them.
- They are experiencing relationship friction with their co-parent, spouse, or partner because they have different views on how they should parent their children.
- They feel their kids don't respect or care about them. They feel taken advantage of and worry that they've raised entitled, spoiled kids.

Until now, the lion's share of advice available to parents addresses these issues at the level of behavior.

The miracle of Peaceful Parenting is that when we shift how we are showing up as parents, the behaviors that drive us bananas often disappear. No sticker charts required.

After embracing Peaceful Parenting, Allyn describes the joy of watching her two children play together, support each other and be there for one another. There are none of the rivalries she experienced with her brother. There is strength in her belief that while her children are still young, she has no reason to believe these strong relational foundations will shift. Her kids are very likely going to be friends for life.

Same here. My children truly love each other. They are in high school, just a year apart, and seem to be able to navigate for themselves the balance between giving each other space in their friend groups and enjoying each other's company. They are each other's biggest cheerleaders, applauding grades well-earned and dreams pursued.

Jenny and Chris have adult children now, and they both gush with joy about their grown children. They speak to the love they experience when spending time together and how their kids call to talk to them—yes, when they have challenges to face, but also when they read a good book or want to talk about Buddhism, politics, or a new romance.

Katie shared a dinner-table conversation with her eight-year-old. She shared stories of her "mean grandmother" and some of the experiences that left her feeling less-than, not good enough, and unworthy. (Yes, we talk about these things in Peaceful Parenting!). Her daughter said, "Well, it sounds like your grandmother didn't know how to be nice to you." Such wisdom.

Daisy shares that as the oldest in her large family, she was responsible for raising her younger siblings. She's been mama-ing for most of her life. She is doing the work of breaking generational patterns that saw little value in affection. It's still hard for her, at times, to express affection for her children, and she is working through learning to give a simple hug. But her daughter? Her daughter came home from school recently and said, "Mama, I think I want to be a therapist."

"Why?" asked Daisy.

"Because my friends all tell me about their feelings. They tell me how lucky I am to have a mother who understands feelings. They want to have a mother like you." Gulp.

Here's the thing about kids. They are just like us. They want to belong. They want to get along. They want to enjoy their time with us, their parent. They want to feel good.

When we give them what they need, they will naturally and easily give us what we need.

The shift to Peaceful Parenting creates a family system where all feelings and needs matter. As parents, we also get to have feelings and needs. We get to take five minutes when we need them.

Children (and adults, if we're being honest) are shouting with their actions and behavior. When we hear them, they no longer need to shout. So magical? Yes. Theoretical? No.

It's simply how brains, emotions, and behaviors work. It's not rocket science—it's human science!

Creating a family that values communication, open emotional expression, and fun is the prescription we need to solve some of life's most significant modern challenges.

Really. And it is the cure to so much that ails us. So much of the conversation around what is going wrong is looking at the symptoms. But when we zoom out, we can see that these challenges stem from how we treat children.

Addiction, for example, is how people numb their feelings of anxiety, inadequacy, and isolation. Addiction is not just about drugs or alcohol. Addiction is looking to an external source of self-medicating that causes harm. Spending, being a workaholic, high-risk sexual behavior, and social media scrolling are some others that can become destructive forces in our relationships. Children raised with a connection to their parents are less likely to experience addiction.

Codependency, the toxic relationship pattern where we rely on the attention, validation, and direction of others to access feelings of self-worth and belonging, is practically the norm in our culture. When internally resourced with a sense of self-worth and belonging, we can enjoy mutually satisfying relationships while maintaining a sense of healthy independence.

Ideology is tearing apart families and communities. Whether political, religious or otherwise, the us-versus-them culture creates inflexible thinking that separates us from each other. As we learn to access empathy and to sit in uncomfortable situations, and then teach our children to do the same, we can find more connections with most people than not.

Materialism, debt, and the harm we cause our planet's natural resources are all outcomes of people wanting more, more, MORE to project a version of themselves to others or fill an empty hole in their inner experience. I could go on, but I hope you'll see that so much of what we face in our world is a crisis of disconnection. So we have to start valuing connection over obedience, guidance over criticism, and doing the brave work of learning a new language...

Of connection, cooperation, and collaboration.

A WORD ON MENTAL HEALTH:

Some topics we explore in these pages can be TRIGGERING.

In many ways, we need to mourn the childhood we didn't have to be the parent for our child that we wish we had.

Whether you experienced emotional wounding, physical trauma, or mental, sexual, or physical abuse as a child, it can be painful to recall the experiences that created our defense mechanisms, emotional reactivity, and conditioned behaviors we exhibit when under stress.

It's ok to feel sad, angry, or resentful. It's crucial to this work that you learn how to handle these things without causing harm to yourself or others. But if it's lingering, festering, or taking you to a place where you don't feel safe, please seek professional support.

We get to heal our emotional and mental health for ourselves and our kiddos. This is why we do what we do! You may consider working with a mental health expert or seek out a parenting coach.

Therapists improve mental health. There are many different therapy modalities, from cognitive behavior therapy to gestalt. If you need help with a mental health issue that you are facing, do your research and get referrals. Therapy is about healing from the experiences of your past.

Coaching isn't diagnostic. Coaching provides a container for learning new skills and the accountability to put them into practice to create the future you want for yourself and your children.

CHAPTER ONE

It's time for a Parenting (R)evolution

When I was 14, I was sitting on my half-brother's bed, looking through the adjoining bathroom door. My step-mom, his mother, was holding his head over the sink and washing his mouth out with a bar of soap. Literally. The bar was so big that he gagged. There was a bottle of tabasco on the toilet cover, waiting to add some extra oomph to his punishment.

He was six. His transgression? Acting like a six-year-old boy.

I loved my baby brother. I'd been an only child until he came along when I was eight. He was magical. Annoying sometimes, sure. But he delighted me. He played with wild abandon. He had a sparkly soul.

As he got older and the harsh and erratic punishments continued, I watched that sparkle dim. He became serious. And eventually sad. By the time he entered high school, he was smoking weed. He didn't have many friends. He stopped caring, about school, about himself, and seemingly, about life.

His mom had extinguished his sparkle.

✳

When we say children are the key to our future, everyone nods. It's simply true. But we often treat them as less-than. We invite you here to honor children more deeply by working to become parents who allow them to realize their greatest, happiest potential.

The obvious evidence that it might be time to evolve how we parent to change the world doesn't come from observing children. It comes from looking at adults. We don't need to look far to see parenting's impact on people. For example, too many of us don't know how to disagree peacefully. We use material possessions to measure worth—even character and wisdom. We reflexively judge and dismiss those who aren't "like us." We stay in unfulfilling jobs and relationships because we fear risk or failure.

Far too many of us have lost our essential connection to joy, creativity, pleasure, and passion because, when we were kids, we got a message that we shouldn't expect too much from life. We should fit in first and foremost, stop crying, and do as we're told by others, by society and culture, and by the relentless pressure for conformity. We should be quiet, still, and just run with the herd.

This is not how to raise leaders who will change the world. This is not how we honor knowing that our children are the key to our future.

To raise happier humans with the courage and self-image to be risk-takers, change-makers, and creators, we need to redefine our roles as parents. Because, let's face it, traditional parenting suggests to most young people that, in some greater scheme of things, their feelings don't matter, they should play it safe, and that many of their dreams are invalid or impractical.

This is not the way to raise future adults who believe in the endless possibilities of being alive, who desire to—and do—effect positive social change.

Just because something's "traditional" or "normal" doesn't mean it's right.

I used to be apprehensive when speaking about parenting (thus my hesitancy about writing this book). I didn't want anyone to feel bad or judged. And I didn't want to be perceived as some sanctimonious know-it-all telling other people how to raise their children.

But, I came to understand Peaceful Parenting. And its universality. And freedom from sanctimony and judgment.

Many years ago, I told my team at the Jai Institute for Parenting that we only needed to reach people who already knew, or felt in their souls, that they wanted to parent peacefully but didn't know how.

"Families know what's best for their children," was the thinking. If someone chooses a more traditional approach, "Well, ok, but I guess they just aren't our crowd."

But no longer. Peaceful Parenting is, we believe, for everyone who cares about children and our collective future.

Recently, we overhauled our curriculum and dove in, up to our eyes, ears, and brains, in the most contemporary psychological and developmental research. We interviewed dozens and dozens of parents. We heard stories from their childhoods. Stories that sometimes broke our hearts.

Heck, *my* childhood story breaks my heart. It's why I founded this institute—so I can do and be better for my children and help others do the same through my overall passion for the coaching profession.

It's the rare person who wasn't somehow wounded by their parents. Not because our parents didn't love us or want to do right by us, but because of pervasive, long-held ideas about good parenting. For example, that good parenting has children meet some prescribed, simple standard of behavior. This means kids are scolded, admonished, shamed back into line, and if they don't comply, punished and, in the worst cases, physically harmed.

Our culture tells us this is good parenting, which causes an internal struggle in parents like us who long for something different. We're uneasy with the commonplace truism that we need to parent our children authoritatively while feeling—and ignoring or suppressing—the strong instinct that it hurts them and us.

When children experience harm, even unintentionally, from the people they love the most, it impacts their self-image and self-esteem. So when we yell at kids or withhold affection because they're "too much," or if we punish them or compel them to stop crying . . . we're doing the same thing to our kids that our parents did to us . . . Who were doing the same thing done to them. And back through the generations we go, one after the next, getting bruised, inside and out.

Ouch.

Especially now. Children today face seismic instability, born into a world that, through a constant barrage of news and media, instills in them the idea they're not safe. Whether it's climate change, media, the pandemic, etc., the culture is doing a number on our kids.

They need *us* to transcend "normal parenting" now.

There are so many examples in life of things everyone thought were "normal" and "fine" that we now see differently.

Cigarettes, for example. The first research that connected smoking with cancer came out in the 1940s. Then the famous, widely discussed Surgeon General's Warning came out in the 1960s.

How did people respond? By puffing away.

It's not a short list. It's human nature. Cocaine was sold in the Sears Roebuck catalog as a cure for sinusitis. For generations, and as recently as the 1970s, autism was considered the result of "frigid mothering." Children were removed from their homes and institutionalized. Many of our mothers smoked and drank alcohol freely through pregnancy. Divorced fathers had no presumptive right to see their kids. Women couldn't have bank accounts.

The point is, we as a species get wiser over time, and discard, often with horror, previously common notions that were considered healthy and wise for ages. And along the way, inertia and a very human suspicion of change maintained the status quo even when the status quo caused harm.

In our work as coaches, we'll hear that a co-parent, when invited into a conversation about punishments and threats, often will say: "Well, I was parented that way, and I'm fine." But I question that, because are we? Are we fine? Do we trust ourselves and others? Can we communicate our feelings and needs without blame, shame, or guilt? Can we feel empathy for the experiences of the people we love?

Hopefully, this book can be a wake-up call for those ready to accept a difficult truth:

"Normal" parenting can cause lifelong emotional harm and damage the best-intentioned, long-term relationships we aspire to with our children.

Parenting has lasting implications for our children's ability to form secure attachments, healthy relationships, and a solid sense of self: self-esteem, self-worth, and self-awareness.

Traditional parenting keeps us from enjoying parenting, having more fun with our kids, and maintaining a lifelong close relationship. It pits siblings against each other. And often makes one parent into the "bad guy."

So why do so many keep parenting this way? Why does what I'm saying here strike so many as shocking?

For one thing, so many people and institutions tell us everything is fine. We're *supposed* to wound, er, discipline our children in the name of their future success. Build scar tissue or something like that. (We'll deeply explore this fallacy in this book.)

We unintentionally continue practices and beliefs that end up hurting our children. They are ingrained in our culture. They have been passed down without much thought or inquiry for generations. And when we question them or wonder if we're doing right by our kids, the world (or our well-meaning neighbor) will tell us that this is simply what good parents do. Good parents discipline their children.

Every day we talk to parents who are desperate, *desperate* to stop yelling at their kids. They want to learn how to parent differently because they *feel* they are close to the line where their parenting is causing harm. Inspiringly, they *want* to do better, aren't meeting the expectations they have for themselves, and want help.

But still. They yell at their kids. I mean, heck! The little buggers make us *crazy*. They're exhausting. They don't listen. And we lose it.

We dismiss their sorrow. We can't handle our inner pain, so how can we handle theirs?

We push them to achieve what we deem to be in their best interest. I mean, our kids need to make us look like good parents! Right?

"It's all just part of being a parent!"

But does it have to be? (I'll cut to the chase. No. It does not.)

And also, I am aware . . .

A parent may not know. He may not know what happens inside a toddler's brain when they're having a tantrum and he yells at them.

A parent may not contemplate what happens to her teenager's self-worth when she isn't trusted.

A parent may not understand the nervous system implications of chronic stress (or even that this is happening to their kids because they're terrified of Mom losing her temper or Dad barking at them to "stop bothering him").

Most parents are simply (understandably) getting by day-to-day, being more patient some days than others, and doing a lot of what was done to them by their parents, even when they promised themselves they wouldn't.

It doesn't have to be that way.

Kids deserve better because they aren't alright.

I know some people aren't going to like this book because *"kids these days are spoiled, entitled, lazy . . . and it's because we don't discipline them!"* (We'll address this more in a moment).

At Jai, we respectfully disagree. There's too much at stake.

Today there's a global children's mental health crisis. Children are committing suicide at an alarming and increasing rate. There's an opioid epidemic and school shootings. And a whole lot of fear is going around, for good reasons.

We're experiencing a collective crisis of disconnection.

Our kids are lost. Of course, they lose themselves in their screens and social media when all they get from the world is panic, fear, anger, grief, and pressure.

So they need us now, more than ever. They need us to be their safe harbor, mentor and guide through the complexities of modern life. They need a place to be vulnerable and feel connected and safe. If not with us, with whom?

And they really deserve to fly the nest with their mental health as intact as possible, feeling supported, seen, known, and loved—*no matter what*—by you.

It is time to transform the way we parent from "normal" parenting to Peaceful Parenting.

This *is* a revolution, albeit a peaceful one. Because we love kids, we'll go to the mat to keep them safe. You love your kid(s). Of course, you do. And so let's be here, together, shoulder to shoulder, arm in arm, heart to heart, and change the way we parent. Let's get better at it and do better for our kids. So they can do better for their future kids. Let's be the generation that breaks the cycles of harm that have perpetuated so many bad things for far too long. This IS a revolution. And an evolution. We know better. So we can do better.

"When a parent heals themselves, they heal their children's children."

❋

AN IMPORTANT NOTE

Peaceful Parenting is NOT permissive parenting.

Let me repeat in all caps:

PEACEFUL PARENTING IS NOT PERMISSIVE PARENTING.

I feel better now.

In many ways, Peaceful Parenting is more challenging than traditional parenting because we aren't instilling fear or using control to enforce compliance (more on this later).

Peaceful Parenting means that we get to do the work of discovering our own emotional regulation, fostering effective communication, and understanding our wants and needs so that we become the model for our children to do the same.

Peaceful Parenting requires us to determine our family values and teach them to our children so that they have a compass of morality to guide their decisions through life.

This takes commitment and practice. It takes presence.

There's a widely held misconception that if we aren't punishing our children, yelling at them, or if, G-d forbid, they have a meltdown at the family reunion, we are too permissive in our parenting. Others tell us we will end up with spoiled, manipulative children who aren't prepared for the "real world."

We will get into this in-depth, but Peaceful Parenting is still very much parenting. It is practicing and modeling the kind of person you hope your child will be when they grow up. It means we are going humbly to acknowledge that we might not be living up to the behaviors, decisions, and actions that we demand our children meet.

(Case in point: How many times have you yelled at your kids to stop yelling? Or maybe you're super-duper evolved and righteous-y like me, and you tell yourself you don't do that, but… you do. I sure do. In some way, we all exhibit hypocrisy as parents.)

Peaceful Parenting includes rules, limits, and boundaries. It honors family values and priorities. Peaceful parents get to say *no*.

Boiling the shift down to its simplest terms, with Peaceful Parenting, we are replacing yelling, punishments, threats, and consequences with communication. Communication doesn't hurt kids. Authentic feelings expressed healthily do not hurt kids.

We aren't abdicating responsibility as a parent by embracing Peaceful Parenting!

Quite the opposite. We claim full responsibility for our actions, words, and deeds. We grow ourselves up so that we can grow our kids up. We immerse ourselves in their world, their needs, and their evolution. We become their partner in growth and maturing.

The ironic truth is that the very parenting practices that well-meaning strangers tell us we need to use to get our kids under control often cause the misbehavior, rebellion, lack of respect, and entitlement that kids are accused of every day. (And really, has there been a generation of kids that haven't been labeled this way by the generation that preceded them?)

The truth? They don't love us less when we scold, criticize, punish, or demean our kids.

They love themselves less.

And grown-ups who don't love themselves are doing an awful lot of harm to our world. There's enough false empowerment going around to drown us all. Real empowerment lives on regardless of external circumstances.

As you explore these concepts, I ask that you keep an open mind and remain willing to question your own experience, thoughts, and actions (with grace, ok? No self-flagellation required).

Doing this work is so important.

Because children raised in a peaceful environment are not spoiled, entitled, lazy, ungrateful, or any of those scary things we fear they might become. They are extraordinary, not because they are better, smarter, or more capable than anyone else, but because they were given the gift of the real and rare experience of unconditional love and radical acceptance by the person they love and admire the most . . . YOU.

Children who receive unconditional love and radical acceptance develop intrinsic motivation based on shared values. They thrive.

KALYJA, AGE 25

How are you aware that the way you've been parented is different than your peers?

I am aware of the difference between how I was parented and my peers in relationship to respect and transparency, which feel like they go hand in hand.

The example coming to mind is the way my mama has always implemented a safe and open space for conversations about sex, intimacy, self-love, and puberty.

Quite literally, making these topics as normalized and honest as our dinner table conversations. As an adult, I look around and feel the huge divide in my community around these same topics due to the glaring lack of education and honesty. The most common thing I hear is "my mom never taught me anything about sex" or "my parents just shamed me."

This rings as something I am deeply grateful for experiencing in her parenting style as it supports us (as her children) to embody confidence, trust in our bodies, and a healthy relationship to honesty and sexuality from day one.

My mama meets our individual stages of life with rights of passages, and overall I still reflect on those moments as fundamental stepping stones in my existence where I got a taste of what it meant to be supported and held accountable simultaneously. The difference in my experience from my peers is while everyone experiences rights of passage naturally, it is rare to truly be honored as an individual for your own growth and development. Ultimately I think this, too, reinstates a sense of belonging and feeling held in the world.

What is the biggest difference this has made in your relationship with your parents or your life?

My mama respects me enough to give me the full truth of her experience without coating it with alternative agendas. This allows me to have my own experience and feel seen as who I am.

Many of my friends' families shy away from these big conversations that are points of connection and the glue of intimate relationships. Our connectivity and depth are the profound results of being very vulnerable, and her teaching me how to show up for life by doing so herself.

What would you want parents thinking about not using punishments or consequences with their kids to know?

In my experience, punishments have created stories for which I have spent most of my adult life in therapy. Reflecting on the simplest of changes from my mama yelling at me as a child to her asking questions with my sister, who is 20 years younger, in the same situation.

This shift makes my sister curious about her process rather than attune to someone else's being "okay." A punishment to keep your child safe, or on track, or "right" is only ever going to create a system of value, a feeling of being enough or never enough.

Regardless, my body has a memory of punishment that has condemned my authentic expression in life.

What differences do you notice between the relationship you have with your parent(s) and the relationship of your friends who were parented more traditionally by their parents?

Connection versus acquaintance.

My mama has made space for any and every part of me to exist AND holds me accountable to my highest self while embodying her authenticity, which is different from mine.

In my surroundings, I witness my friends' familial differences cause voids and communication breakdowns that evolve into dismissal. I am so grateful for the honest connection and ritual that my mama has gifted me in life by valuing and demonstrating it herself.

CHAPTER TWO

What Do You Really Actually Want for Your Kids?

Growing up in Texas in the 1980s, Allyn's childhood was vastly different from her mother's. Like so many parents, her mother desperately wanted to ensure that her daughter never had to endure the horrible things she experienced as a child.

Allyn's mom experienced physical threats and the unfair responsibility of caring for her two younger brothers. Her mom told her awful stories, like being chased with weapons as a child or watching her mother fall asleep while cigarettes burned away by her side, too afraid to wake her up.

Allyn had it better than her mom. She wasn't chased around the house. She wasn't beaten. She was often reminded of how "good she had it." It shocked her when she found herself at a breaking point, sitting in a therapist's office in her twenties, overwhelmed by her work as a first-year teacher.

Much to Allyn's surprise, her therapist kept returning to questions and reflections about Allyn's mom and the emotional experiences Allyn had (and didn't have) as a child.

Allyn felt disoriented by the direction of the conversation. On paper, she had achieved all the right accomplishments in her life. She got good grades, went to a great college, and received an impressive degree. She'd been the consummate "good girl." However, when choosing what college she would attend, Allyn recalls that her main criterion was that the campus was beyond the borders of her home state.

Allyn's parents' goals for their kids were that they become successful and independent and don't rely on their parents for anything after they leave home. Her mom truly believed she gave her daughter everything she needed to meet these goals.

Eventually, Allyn acknowledged that her deepest desire was for someone (anyone!) to tell her what to do in her life. She had always gotten every answer, direction, and final decision from her mother. When she went to college, she looked to friends for answers and guidance. She entered relationships with partners who were happy to decide for her. Today, she continues to practice stepping into her power as a wife, mother, and business owner.

Allyn realized she'd been living her life by doing exactly what other people told her to do. In her early years, her mother made every decision for her. When she went to college, she followed the crowd, taking the classes her friends suggested and joining the sorority they chose. She later chose a life partner who was happy to decide for her as well, a dynamic they are currently working to shift in their marriage.

When Allyn had children, she didn't think much about the long-term relationship she wanted to have with them. It didn't occur to her to discover who they were as unique individuals. Allyn fell into a common parenting role: ensuring her children behaved, participated in the "right" activities, and achieved success in school and athletics. But in her heart, Allyn wanted her children to become the truest versions of themselves. She didn't want them to experience life, as she had, at the mercy of what other people thought.

After Allyn's breakthroughs with her therapist, she realized that she wanted something different for her children than what she thought made a "good parent." She was determined to change to be the best mom she could be for her kids. Allyn wanted to have the kind of relationship with her children that didn't leave them wanting to get as far away from her as possible at the earliest opportunity. She re-prioritized the relationship between her and her children, placing connection over meeting her expectations (or society's) of what was right (or wrong) for them. Today she continues to step into her power as a wife, mother, and business owner.

Allyn decided to raise her children with connection, authenticity, family values, and a deep understanding of her own needs and theirs. This is when she found Jai. Allyn is hopeful for a future where she will continue to have a connected, loving relationship with her children as they enter adulthood. She expects to be a supportive and active part of their lives for their whole lives. And she hopes that more than any other goal she has as a parent, that they know themselves what they want for their lives and what they don't.

It never occurred to me, either. I didn't stop and think about what I wanted for myself and my kids as a parent. I just birthed those babies and thought I'd know what to do! Many of us bring children into the world and operate on autopilot until a crisis has us questioning everything.

When we ask parents what they want for their kids, most give pretty similar answers. They want their kids to be happy. They want them to be productive members of society and find a level of success that allows them to live comfortable lives. However, these don't tell us very much about what we *really, actually* want for our kids or our experience of raising them.

Happy? What does that even mean?

Successful? Based on what measure?

Comfortable? According to what standard?

The potentially more challenging concept to consider is how the tactics, relational skills, and parenting strategies that we use daily impact our children's ability to have these vaguely defined future experiences.

How might we consider the relationship within the context of human needs? *What do our children want and need from us? What do we want and need from our children? What do we want our future relationship with our children to be? Are the ways that we are interacting with our children today leading us closer to or further away from that future vision?*

Let's look closely at the objective of traditional parenting. It eliminates or minimizes annoying, irritating, and harmful behavior using power-over strategies (or the equally damaging strategy of under-parenting, meaning throwing in the towel and giving them the iPhone.) The emphasis is on short-term behavior modification strategies that make life easier in the moment. But parents often haven't considered how these short-term behavior modification strategies impact the child and the parent-child relationship over the long term.

Power-over strategies rely on our bigger size, our harsh voice, or our actual power to demand and enforce compliance to rules, limits, and boundaries. As adults, we can send children to their rooms, take their toys away, not drive them to their friend's houses, or force them to sit in a time-out. We have all of the power in the relationship.

Power-under strategies mean withholding affection, emotional abandonment, and an abdication of parental responsibilities.

Even parents committed to Peaceful Parenting resort to power-over strategies like yelling, threatening, or punishing when they haven't learned new strategies to cope with parenting's more stressful moments. Despite a commitment to break these generational patterns, staying calm is hard when everything feels like chaos.

We lose it because we are tired, stressed, and irritated. We are desperate for a break. We don't think we have another option. We also don't think. Because when we are in a state of fight, flight, or freeze, we lose access to the areas of our brain that are responsible for reasoning and strategic thinking.

Here's my dirty little secret: When my kids were young, my go-to expert for parenting advice was the Super Nanny, who, as you may know, promotes timeouts and enforced apologies as a primary behavior modification strategy. First of all, the show made me feel better about myself: *"Phew, at least things aren't that out of control in my house!"* And secondly, the show normalized timeouts as "peaceful punishments," promising they could easily curb the chaos of having two toddlers in the house.

If you remember, the Super Nanny's advice was to sit your child in a designated time-out spot for the same number of minutes as their age. At the end of the time-out, they needed to apologize. If they didn't, they would repeat the time-out until they complied by saying, "I'm sorry."

So one day, when my son was four, he did something bad. Who knows what? He was four. Probably he bashed his sister over the head with a block. That happened a lot. Anyway, we did the Super Nanny thing, and I'm not kidding. He was on the time-out step for well over an hour. We are talking over fifteen rounds of making him sit there, asking for an apology, him refusing, and then sitting there again.

I crumbled. For the rest of the day, he wouldn't look at me.

The insanity of this idea hit *me* like a woodblock over the head. *"I'm taking actions that are hurting my relationship with my son. He doesn't trust me because I just did something awful. And how the heck am I going to teach him not to hit if he doesn't like me or trust me?"*

Now, I'm sure if I'd continued down this path, there would eventually have been some punishment that created the desired outcome, but at what cost?

Because here's the rub: Power-over strategies "work."

Children will eventually comply when rules are enforced through punishments. Power-over, dominant, or authoritative strategies meet their desired goals. Negative behaviors are eliminated. Positive behaviors are enforced. Given the pressure we feel to have our kids prove what good parents we are through their "good" behavior, it's no wonder that we do whatever it takes to condition our children to comply.

Traditional parenting is . . . traditional. It's the way it's always been done. It wasn't too long ago that children worked the family farm or the local factory. The expectation that we can transcend the quality of life of the family we were born into is a very modern idea. Learning to stifle creativity, follow the rules, and comply with authority were necessary to survive in many circumstances in past generations.

But the world has changed. Modern times require collaboration, innovation, and courage. Not compliance.

A big turning point for me was considering the responsibility of raising a daughter. If I scared her, threatened her, or forced her into doing what I wanted her to do, when and how, exactly, would she learn to stand her ground when the next (bigger, scarier, more powerful) person demanded something from her?

. . . The friend who wanted her to join in drinking or drug use

. . . The boy who wanted her to have sex before she was ready

. . . The boss who wanted her to breach her sense of integrity

When we deeply consider what traditional parenting teaches our children about themselves and the world, it kind of boggles the mind. Traditional parenting tells us that our children should obey us, make their wants and needs subservient to the adults in their lives, stay quiet, never be mad, sad, or scared, and by all means, not ever do anything that might make their family look anything less than perfect. And children who learn to comply become adults who comply. Or demand compliance from others.

THE BELIEFS OF TRADITIONAL PARENTING

Chris was the "good little girl." She learned to obey because if she didn't, she would get in trouble: *"Big trouble . . . really, really big."* She was often spanked, which obviously left a mark (pun intended). But she shared that the fear, worry, and anxiety she felt about what would happen if she got caught misbehaving was worse than the actual physical punishment.

Chris recalls being terrified when her older sister got in trouble in high school. Her sister lost her privileges for the entire summer. She couldn't use the phone. She couldn't go out. She was basically (Chris's words) the house slave.

So Chris decided that she would be really, really good, which made her really, really fearful. Her fear followed her into adulthood. She is only now learning, in her fifties, that she gets to have feelings and needs and ask for what she wants. She's learning to take up more space and say hard things. She shares, *"Why would I ever want to do that to my kids?"*

We've been living with a huge misunderstanding: Obedience is the path to respect. Of course, we want our kids to behave in ways that benefit others and the greater good. But the old paradigm wrongly assumes that children won't make "the right" decisions from their internal sense of right and wrong, so we must demand that they obey. This is simply not true. We aren't (paradoxically) giving *them* enough respect.

This doesn't mean we don't provide guidance, explanation, or contextual course correction when appropriate. We are still here to teach our children about the world around them and help them to navigate it with integrity, morality, and ethics.

When we teach our kids that they need to obey authority without question, we teach them that compliance is more important than integrity. We teach them not to trust themselves. We create children, teens, and adults who look outward, instead of inward, for answers about what to do and how to act. Their decisions rely on external forces of authority throughout their lives. Adults who allow others to dictate their actions and choices end up feeling lost, inauthentic, and unfulfilled. They enter relationships and careers where they don't have a voice or feel like they don't have a choice. We raise the next generation of people-pleasers and bullies.

No one *wants* this for their children. Instead, let's consider the long-term outcomes we want for our children, how they can best embody their sense of self, how we can teach them to make good decisions, and how empowered they feel to take action based on what is best for their lives. Because I think what we *really, actually want* for our kids is to be self-directed, not other-directed.

THE THREE UH-O'S OF TRADITIONAL PARENTING: OBLIGATION, OPTICS, AND OWNERSHIP

Obligation

Ashley grew up in the Hindu tradition, a culture that emphasizes reverence toward your elders. This was an inviolable value in her family. Regardless of the circumstance, the expectation was that children respect and defer to their elders. As an adoptee, her parents expected her to feel ingratiated to them for "taking her in." She got the message: she owed her family deference and obligation.

As a child, she was often demeaned and belittled for her disrespect. Her parents lacked emotional availability, dismissed her feelings, and shut down her emotional expression. She struggled with her relationship with her parents into her adulthood. Ashley often found herself in situations with her family that compromised her sense of self, even as an adult.

This experience is not exclusive to Ashley's family or culture. The traditional model of parenting values conditioned behavior over connection, safety, and mutual respect between parents and children. It's no wonder many of us can't wait to move away, create new lives, and limit contact with our parents as adults.

Three years ago, Ashley reached a breaking point with her mother. When Ashley's three-year-old daughter returned home from a long and tiring day at preschool, she was very excited to see her grandma. Ashley's daughter burst into the room, a ball of energy, ready to share everything that happened at school. Ashley could tell that her daughter was on the cusp of losing it, but her mom was upset that she didn't "properly" greet her first.

Ashley's mom expected her granddaughter to behave with deference and formality, just as she'd expected Ashley to do when she was young.

Ashley tried to convey to her mom that her daughter was tired and hungry and just needed a moment, but Ashley's mom wouldn't hear it.

She lashed out at Ashley, saying, "You're not doing a good job raising your children." She continued to criticize her. "You have not taught them to behave properly." Ashley hit her limit. She took a brave stand and made a powerful choice. She asked her mother to leave her house. Their relationship has never recovered.

This pivotal moment gave Ashley a profound sense of conviction to become the parent she wanted to be for her children, the parent she wished she'd had. She wrote a new story for herself and her kids.

Traditional parenting says if we provide for our children, they owe us, no matter how we treat them. This does not create the conditions for a mutually beneficial relationship. We were told we owe our parents for putting a roof over our heads and food on the table. Giving life is often used as a "you owe me" framework, which creates resentment.

We might simply look to our own relationships with our parents to see how this plays out. If you were lucky enough to have parents who did not communicate this expectation, I'd guess you are close to people whose parents did. The truth? Children didn't ask to be born. We brought them into the world. The responsibility? It's all ours.

Only through creating connected, loving relationships with our children that welcome our needs, values, and desires will we forge truly reciprocal relationships that last into adulthood and beyond. Ultimately, we all want to have our children in our lives because they want to be, not because they are obligated.

Optics

Jenny grew up in the Midwest with parents who were intent on living the white picket fence dream. Everything had to look perfect. All the time. Jenny was to keep any problems, challenges, or upsets in the family to herself. No one was to know that anything was less than rosy at her house.

Jenny had to behave in a way that reflected well on her family. She felt that she needed to be a walking billboard for the projection of success that mattered to her family. She interpreted this to mean that she mattered less than what other people thought. Not surprisingly, Jenny developed a rebellious streak. The pressure to be outwardly successful, regardless of what was going on behind closed doors, became so intolerable that she lashed out with her actions as a teenager. She started drinking in the eighth grade, dyed her hair green and purple, and covered her body in piercings. She became sexually promiscuous and exhibited high-risk behavior. Her inner child was screaming, "Take THAT, perfect parents!"

Traditional parenting puts the onus on children to make their parents look good. Children's behavior is a direct reflection of the worthiness of their parents. Traditional parents don't often look at their children's ability to empathize with others or speak up in the face of injustice. They don't speak of their kindness. They want the trophies to display on the mantle. Self-worth and self-esteem are less important than the image presented by the child.

How did we get to a place where optics are more important to us than the truth? How can we expect our children, or ourselves for that matter, to live lives of integrity and fulfillment if we're focused only on the external representations of our lives? How do we begin to show our children the beauty of holding duality, the both-and of the whole messy, complicated truth of being human if we expect them only to show other people the "good stuff?" And why, pray tell, do we care so much about what other people think?

Generations of parents have unconsciously carried on this harmful tradition of performative living. When our children arrive in the world, from the very beginning, they cry too loud on planes, have embar-rassing meltdowns in the aisles of stores, and talk back to us at family functions, exposing the truth that we are not perfect and that they have opinions about it. The only remedy is to require them to hide their feel-ings and true selves, suppress their needs, and lie to the world about our flaws (and theirs!).

In asking them to take on the enormous and inappropriate task of representing us, we invite them to join us in cultivating their shame, secrecy, and disconnection. If they reject our demands, we remove our love and approval and rob them of their sense of belonging.

Only when we can accept the fullness of our humanity, feelings, and transgressions can we remove this oppressive responsibility from our kids' shoulders so they can be free to become all they are here to be, mistakes and all.

Ownership

My mom was a 1970s feminist powerhouse. A newspaper editor at twenty-five, she was a professional trailblazer in every sense of the word, like Mary Tyler Moore with a baby under one arm and an attaché case under the other. Her brilliance was matched in equal parts by her charm, beauty, and unrelenting ambition. Naturally, she wanted every-thing for me.

Everything included getting top grades, attending dance lessons at the most competitive studios in NYC, landing every theater role I audi-tioned for, and doing it all with an unwavering smile on my face.

So, I tap-danced through childhood (literally and figuratively), feeling like my life depended on it. From my perspective, my mom's bragging about my achievements felt like she was claiming responsibility for them. It seemed that my accomplishments bolstered her confidence, which caused me, as a teen, to resent mine. I became unmotivated. I underperformed my potential, because I didn't want to give her the satisfaction. This hurt my mom. And, of course, it hurt me in the long run too.

Traditional parenting tells us we are not only responsible for our children, but we also own them and their accomplishments. Parents are encouraged, even celebrated, for making decisions for their kids, from what they eat and wear, to their interests, life, and career choices. If our kids succeed, it's because of the opportunities we gave them. If they fail to live up to the life we imagined for them, they have failed us.

Without a sense of ownership over their lives, how can we expect our children to feel connected to what brings them joy and purpose? How can we expect them to put in the hard work it takes to succeed if what they're working toward has nothing to do with their own choices? We can't.

Traditional parenting confuses taking ownership of another person's life with helping, guiding, and supporting them to experience *their* best life. We owe our children the best version of *ourselves*. We owe them the opportunity to make their own choices and to learn from their mistakes. Our children have the right to change their minds and figure out who they are in the world without worrying about losing our love, support, and approval.

How, exactly, do we expect children to learn to become responsible adults? We lament young adults heading back to their parents after they graduate or being difficult employees, but did they even have a chance? We teach children to keep their needs and feelings to themselves. We micromanage (parent-splain) every decision they make and then wonder why they can't fend for themselves when they leave home. It's as if we think there's a magical adult switch that will just turn on.

All because we've been living out this crazy idea that our role as parents is to get our kids to behave, regardless of the impact that our efforts to manipulate our children's behavior have on our long-term relationship with our child, their mental health, sense of internal safety, self-confidence and self-esteem.

What's even crazier is that it doesn't really, actually work.

Think back to your childhood and try to call into your memory the person you knew who had the strictest parents (maybe that was you.)

One of two things most likely happened:

1. They rebelled. Big time. They were the head of the pack when it came to breaking the rules, curfews, and expectations. They stopped achieving their goals so that their parents couldn't have the satisfaction of their accomplishments.
2. They complied. Much like Chris's story earlier, they became a projection of their parents' dreams and vision. They stopped believing in themselves, losing sight of who they were along the way.

It is time to examine, question, and redefine what success means for ourselves as parents and our kids as growing humans.

So here's our vision of the redefinition of successful parenting for the modern world. Feel free to borrow, amend, steal or edit. From our perspective, the simple act of considering what you truly want for yourself and your kids beyond society's, culture's, or your family's expectations of what success means is a step in the right direction.

THE THREE YE-S'S OF PEACEFUL PARENTING: SAFETY, SELF-RELIANCE, AND SELF-ACTUALIZATION

Safety

Of course, children's physical safety is a primary responsibility of parenting. And sometimes, keeping our children safe means we will do things that go against our intentions of peace. When a child is running into a road, we are going to yell. It's o.k. Obviously!

Given what we now know about the effects of chronic stress on brain development, it's important to expand the scope of physical safety to include emotional and relational safety.

Creating emotional and relational safety is not about indulging children. It's demonstrating that we are a safe person for our children, regardless of external circumstances. Since most of us didn't experience this in childhood, we need to learn to do this as adults.

Emotional safety is demonstrated through the ability to express all emotions (even anger, fear, or sadness) in a way that does not cause harm to ourselves or others. It is the ability to feel our feelings fully, without numbing, stuffing, or avoiding.

Our children experience emotional safety when they know we won't hurt them when we are angry. They experience emotional safety when we share our grief with them over a loss and don't keep it hidden behind closed doors.

Emotional security emerges from our willingness to be open and honest with our children in an age-appropriate way. Kids can tell when we are stressed, anxious, or afraid, so when we try to hide these things from them, they will make up a whole lot of stories about why we are "off" and, by and large, will assume it's about them. Emotional safety can't exist without our ability to share and express our feelings while remaining grounded and calm. Vulnerability is a peaceful parent's superpower.

Peaceful Parenting requires us to reacquaint ourselves with our feelings and emotions and to stop thinking about emotions as good or bad. Our human experience is so much richer when we allow ourselves to feel. We deny ourselves self-awareness, insight, and discernment when we have an unhealthy expression of any emotion (for example, whether we stuff our anger or explode when we are angry). Guess how our kids learn how to respond to their feelings? You guessed it! They learn from us.

Remember Allyn's story? While Allyn's mom may not have chased her around the house with a gun (unlike her mother), she still exploded in rage and anger. Once, Allyn realized she had forgotten her oboe on her way to her music lesson. Her mom lost it, screaming at her that she had "$%* for brains." While being screamed at, Allyn thought two things: "My mom is nuts, AND I'm a terrible person who has $%* for brains." Allyn was scared. Trust eroded. And guess what: When Allyn had her own kids, she'd find herself yelling her head off, despite her strong desire to do better for her children than was done for her.

Ultimately our children's degree of emotional safety comes from our ability to handle all of their feelings and our own without causing harm. Anger doesn't need to yell or lash out. Sorrow doesn't need to be held in or hidden. Fear doesn't need to be ignored or shamed.

And joy doesn't need to be tamped down or quieted.

> *If you'd like more resources on discovering the tools of emotional safety, access our free training, The Science of Staying Calm, at www.jaiinstituteforparenting.com/ book-resources*

Relational safety is how we feel in our relationships, and most specifically, inside of our most intimate relationships. Do we believe our connections are reliable and trustworthy or are they dangerous and unpredictable?

We've talked about shifting the measure of success in this exploration of Peaceful Parenting away from "good behavior." Many experts in the field claim that "secure attachment" should be our new goalpost.

Secure attachment means that we feel safe in relating to other people. We trust them. And we are trustable. Fundamentally, this is the powerful belief that:

> **We are worthy of love, can receive the love of others,
> and can give love to others without condition.**

(I know, swoon.)

The attachment center in the brain learns to understand relationships through our primary relationship with our parent(s).

Perhaps your inability to tell your partner what you need from her is making more sense now. Perhaps you can find compassion for your conflict avoidance or your need to control the people in your life so they don't abandon you.

The way our parents raised us left a mark. We get to come to terms with this to move forward in our journey toward Peaceful Parenting, which we will discuss in the next chapter. But here's the big deal: Our children's brain's attachment center will be informed and conditioned by their relationship with us.

We are the ones leaving the mark this time.

(Deep breath. It's all going to o.k. It's never too late to repair our relationship with our children. Along the way, I've discovered that there isn't anything that can't be handled, dealt with, and forgiven. You'll read some of the stories of my parenting missteps as you read this book.)

Self-reliance

One of the biggest problems with traditional parenting is that it teaches children to rely on external influences to determine their decisions. Telling a child what to do doesn't teach them why they should do it.

The goal of Peaceful Parenting is to foster and encourage *intrinsic motivation*. This is the desire to do the right thing based on our internal values, knowing how to do what needs to be done, and feeling a sense of accomplishment and purpose through our decisions, actions, and results.

I was recently speaking to a friend of mine who is a college admissions coach, and she shared that alumni who conduct interviews can immediately tell the difference between a candidate who is used to looking to their parents for answers versus a candidate who has the confidence to look inside of themselves for answers.

They prefer the latter.

What we often see is what we call a generational pendulum. So, for example, if you were a latchkey kid whose parents provided food, shelter, and not much else, it is understandable and natural that in your effort to not be like your parents, you become hypervigilant in your parenting.

Since power-under parenting was such a common experience in the '70s and '80s, what we've experienced thematically in the last twenty years is hyper-parenting.

I remember a day when my son was maybe seven years old, and we were playing with a group of kids and moms at a lake. A tree had fallen over and lay perched over the water. My kid loved (and still loves) to climb. I kid you not, when he was just four, I couldn't find him one summer day. The windows were open, letting the lovely New Hampshire summer breeze flow through the house, and as I called to him, I could hear him calling back, but he was nowhere to be found. Finally, I spied him outside a second-story bedroom window, eye to eye with me in a tree. By the time I made it downstairs, he was back on solid ground. Exhale.

Anyway, this day at the beach, he was climbing the tree suspended over the water. Another mom came rushing up to me in a total panic. "Your son! Do you see where he is? You need to get him down from there!! It's dangerous!"

"He's o.k.," I shared. "He can swim, and he knows his limits." I don't think she liked me anymore, but I decided at some point that I would rather my child have a broken arm than a broken spirit.

Self-reliance comes from allowing our children the magical opportunity to figure things out for themselves. Rather than micromanaging them, rescuing them from their mistakes, or telling them exactly how to do a thing, stand back and allow them to do it their way.

In traditional parenting, trust is earned. In Peaceful Parenting, trust is granted. Autonomy is preserved. And children are allowed to figure things out and develop confidence and competence. They are given responsibility and then guided, as needed, to live into their age-appropriate responsibilities.

Self-actualization

Human beings share common needs, whether they are children or adults. We all share the eight core needs:

Safety: Our physiological need for shelter, food, water, physical safety, rest, and emotional well-being.

Variety: The need for excitement, unique experiences, and access to new information and change.

Validation: The desire to be seen, understood, and appreciated by others.

Significance: The need to know we matter and are essential to others.

Connection: The need to give and receive love and feel that we belong to a community.

Autonomy: The need to own the choices and decisions that we make for ourselves.

Growth: The desire to do better, learn more, and gain expertise in the areas of life that matter most to us.

Contribution: The need to be of service to others and make the world a better place.

One of our credos at Jai is that:

**ALL behavior is an expression of a need,
whether it is met or unmet.**

So if we look at traditional parenting through the lens of these core human needs, we can find a clear understanding of children who are exhibiting negative behavior. They are simply using less-than-desirable strategies to get their needs met.

When a child's core needs are met, behavior usually resolves. When a child grows up in an environment where their needs have been honored (most of the time—not any of us are perfect need meet-ers because we have our feelings and needs, too!), they have the opportunity to know themselves honestly. Knowing their passions, purpose, and direction in life leads to self-actualization.

Self-actualization is self-determination. It means we know who we are and what we want. It means we have tremendous access to empathy for others because we don't take their actions or behaviors personally. It means we can take responsibility for our mistakes and failures because we know that we are worthy and lovable despite them. We can take risks. We don't fear failure. We don't fear love. Or the loss of it.

I would say this is what we *really* want for our kids in the modern age. This is what we need them to embody to be the future leaders that our world so desperately needs.

AVA, AGE 6

What do you like the most about how mommy and daddy treat you?

Well, I know you work hard to learn how to be parents.

What do you mean by that?

Like sometimes you make mistakes, and I make mistakes, and that's ok, and no one is perfect, but it's important to clean up our mess. I think that's good. And we talk a lot.

What do we talk about?

Well, anything. We talk a lot! (both laughing) Like our feelings.

What about our feelings?

That they are ok and everyone has them, even if they are scary.

That's right. Have you ever been punished for doing something wrong?

You mean like not cleaning my room?

Sure! Do I punish you for not cleaning your room?

Well, I don't know actually what a punish is, but sometimes you get frustrated. But sometimes we clean my room together. It depends on if you had a long day.

LOL. Yes, I do get frustrated with a messy room. Usually, when it's the end of the day, and I'm tired, huh? And we have a value of taking care of our things, right? Do you get in trouble for not having a clean room?

No, I don't think so. But you usually give me choices.

Like what?

Like you say, "Ava, do you want to pick up ten things each right now or wait until the morning when you have more energy to clean up?"

And what do you usually choose?

The MORNING!

How would you feel if I punished you for not cleaning your room?

Scared . . . Sad . . . Angry!

So you would feel like I don't understand or listen to you, which would make you feel angry and sad and maybe a little scared?

Yes.

I understand that. It's important to feel like I am listening to you.

Yeah.

M: Ok. Next question: How do you know what the rules are?

What are rules? Like not hitting Sasha?

Yes, like our values in our home.

We talk about them.

Do you follow them?

Sometimes, I mean, you don't even follow them all the time.

HA! You are absolutely right. So what do we do when we don't follow the rules?

Ummm, usually we remind each other, and then we have a re-do. That's like when we do it over.

We act it out again, huh? And then we get to practice doing it the way we wished we did it the first time.

Yeah.

Is that fun for you?

Yes! It's AWESOME.

M: Yeah, I like it a lot too. It's never too late to try again.

CHAPTER THREE

Making Peace with Your Parenting Past

As a teenager, Ashley felt so despondent and lost that on two separate occasions, at fourteen and sixteen years old, she attempted to end her own life. Recalling that awful time, she feels pained that she was so alone. Sure, her mother was *in* the hospital building, but rarely in her room with her. Hooked up to an I.V. and drinking vats of liquid charcoal to absorb the toxins from her overdose, Ashley recalls that neither of her parents was by her side to hold her hand, affirm their love, or soothe her.

As Ashley reflected on this pivotal moment in her young life, she realized that she could have held on to her resentment, anger, judgment, and blame. She would be justified in thinking all these years later, "*How could they have done that to me*?" It would be perfectly understandable to feel righteous and tell herself repeatedly how wronged she was by her parents.

But she recognized that would only create more negativity inside her. She understood the importance of holding two or more simultaneous truths about her parents in her heart.

Being alone and scared in a hospital bed was awful. Ashley deserved love, comfort, support, and compassion in those moments. On the other hand, Ashley now recognizes that her mother lacked the character and skills to support her daughter. She came to peace, knowing her mom loved her the best she knew how. Part of Ashley's healing was reconciling that her mother didn't have the tools, insight, or emotional intelligence she needed to show up in the way she needed.

This perspective of grace and forgiveness is the gift that Ashley gives to herself so she can create a different future for her kids.

This is the work of making peace with our parenting past.

"Forgiveness is giving up all hopes of a better past."
~Jack Canfield

Every one of us experienced some level of emotional wounding or harm as a child. Our parents hurt us. We may also have been hurt by our teachers, siblings, peers, or other adults in our lives. This doesn't mean the people who did these things were bad people. By and large, they were simply doing what they could, given what they knew.

Everyone experiences emotional wounding. Even as peaceful parents, our children will experience some level of emotional wounding from us and others. While Peaceful Parenting isn't permissive parenting, it also isn't *perfect parenting*. As humans, we are all messy and complicated.

With perspective, we can often see the gifts in our more challenging experiences as children shaping our boundaries, morality, and values.

Perhaps we developed resilience, grit, or the ability to depersonalize challenges through these experiences. Personal growth requires experiences, reflection, awareness, and integration. We grow *through* life's challenges, not despite them.

Emotional wounding, in and of itself, therefore, is not the problem. The lack of resolution, coherence, and healing of these wounds bears addressing.

The power dynamics most often at the root of the wounding or trauma we experienced *were considered normal*. For most of us, our parents simply did their best given the information, knowledge, and resources they had to be good parents. The experiences we had as children inform our sense of inner safety and security. When we experience a threat to our safety, our psyche develops defense mechanisms. Defense mechanisms are simply ways to protect us from getting hurt again. This makes perfect sense, right? Understandably, we create adaptive mechanisms for our emotional safety, just like we learn adaptive mechanisms for our physical safety (we only need to put our hand on the stove once to learn that it is HOT).

Often, however, it is our emotional defense mechanisms that cause disconnection in our relationships. We'll explore this deeply in Chapter Ten, but for now, it serves our purpose to become aware of how our own childhood experiences created our defenses and how our defenses are impacting our current relationships.

We must distinguish traumatic experiences of violence, assault, and sexual abuse from emotional wounding. If this applies to you, go easy on yourself. (Make sure you are getting the professional assistance you need.) Your defense mechanisms and trauma adaptations were created by your psyche as very wise, intelligent ways of coping with what happened to you. You are innocent, as are your defenses.

When I was a kid, many of my neighbors got the belt as punishment. I remember sitting as quietly as a mouse in my friend Stephanie's kitchen, listening in anguish as her father administered physical punishment. Many years later, I was at my husband's boss's house. His young daughter got in trouble and was brought into his office and given the belt. My whole body burned.

Jenny told us a story of a mom she was coaching who'd recently gone through a divorce. She was working with the mom to embrace the transformational methodology we teach parents, and things were going amazing in the family. But when her boys (three and six) went to their dad's house, he was still spanking them.

One day, as the dad was getting ready to spank the three-year-old, he said, *"Daddy, do you need to spank me? Can't we just have a conversation?"* I mean . . . my heart.

One of our coaches, Lisa Smith, shared a story about working with a dad going through a divorce. The courts will often mandate parent coaching as a condition of custody. This dad grew up in a very authoritative home. He was regularly punished, yelled at, and demeaned. His father demanded obedience, and so he demanded it, too.

"But I'm fine," this dad lamented. "I have a good job. I provide for my family. Discipline is critical, and it's important to me that my kids have discipline! My dad wanted what was best for me. And I want what is best for my kids!"

Gently, Lisa pointed to the glaring blind spot. This dad, who very clearly wanted the best for his children, was not fine. He couldn't keep and maintain healthy relationships. His wife had spent years trying to get him to listen to her and "get it." The more she shared what wasn't working, the more he insisted things were working fine. He had stagnated at work and often felt like a doormat his colleagues climbed over to get jobs for which he should have been the next in line. His kids were scared of him and preferred the softer presence of their mom.

Here's the thing: These were all loving parents who were deeply committed to their kids. They thought they were doing the right thing, parenting, by and large, the way their parents parented them. We are all impacted by generational parenting patterns of the past. Fine may be normal. But it's a pretty low bar for the expectations we have for ourselves and our children.

We can be quite aware of what our parents did to us that we didn't like, but this doesn't mean the experiences aren't impacting our parenting. Without coming to peace with what happened to us as kids, most of the impact of our early emotional wounding or trauma lives underneath the surface of our awareness.

Paradoxically, we sometimes defend the actions of our parents and live in a not-quite-true story about how wonderful they were. We defend their actions or blame ourselves for their mistreatment, telling ourselves that if we were better kids, they wouldn't have had to spank us, abandon us, berate us, or (insert your parents' wounding mechanism here).

When we are stressed, tired, angry, threatened (or perceive that we are being threatened), this unresolved hurt spills out all over the people we love. Perhaps we lash out at our kids, partner or spouse, family or friends. Or maybe we shut down and isolate ourselves (as a way to protect ourselves).

We might project our defenses inward, speaking to ourselves with more judgment and cruelty than we would ever speak to another person. Emotional reactivity—the feeling that we don't have any control over how we act when triggered—is a clear sign that we have unfinished business from our past.

Remember, the goal of Peaceful Parenting is that our children experience secure attachments. But we can't give our children something we don't have ourselves. We need to earn *ourselves* secure attachment if we accept this as the desired goal for our children's healthy development.

The way to do this is to make peace with our parents or the other adults (or children) who caused us emotional harm and even trauma at a young age. These are the emotional wounds that shape our defenses. Our defenses keep us from open, intimate, and aware relationships with the people we love, including our kids.

"Show me where you're resisting joy, and I can see your wounding."

✳

WHY DO WE NEED TO LOOK BACK TO MOVE FORWARD?

"Oh god," Sara said, "do I really need to talk about my parents? I just want my kids to stop bickering."

"I haven't talked to my parents in years!" shared Audrey. "They aren't part of my life, and I don't want them to be. I try not to think about them anymore."

"I'm so close with my mom! Sure, she wasn't perfect, but she did her best and worked hard to give me the best opportunities to have the life she didn't have," shared Nick.

✳

Many of our parents didn't have the capacity to meet our eight core human needs. Because our parents didn't meet these needs, we adapted, often in less than useful ways. For example, if our parents made us feel insignificant, we might spend a lifetime seeking significance externally. We are probably even (unconsciously) asking our children to make us feel significant.

Suppose our parents were never satisfied with our grades or other accomplishments. In that case, we might spend a lifetime seeking external achievement versus inner fulfillment, or we might reject achievement, whole cloth as a way of rejecting the pressure.

If our parents withheld their love and affection, we might fear making mistakes if we are less than perfect. We strive for perfection so the people we love won't leave.

These are just a few examples of how unresolved unmet needs spill into our relationships with our kids in two distinct ways: We either overcorrect and experience the generational pendulum, trying so hard to *not* be like our parents that we create new dysfunctional relationship patterns; or, the wounding lives in our subconscious, and we unconsciously do the same thing to our kids our parents did to us! We question ourselves, shame ourselves, and get stuck in the sabotaging pattern rather than creating a new way of relating that honors our past while paving the way for a new future.

Lina grew up in a "typical" (her word) Asian family. She followed the prescribed path, working in corporate for a few years and then returning to school to earn her MBA. She did everything "right," based on her cultural and familial expectations, until she realized that she was living inauthentically. Now, as a parent, she deeply desires to parent differently than how she was raised. She doesn't want to hit her children or punish or yell at them to have them comply according to prescribed standards or use her children's accomplishments to receive validation for her parenting.

Her intention clear, Lina forged a new path forward. But a new challenge emerged. Was she being too permissive? Providing enough structure? Creating clear boundaries? Through self-reflection, Lina realized she was afraid to "offend" her children. This overcorrection is something Lina now manages day-to-day. Through self-awareness and gently returning to her chosen parenting path, she is supporting herself and her family in a new way of loving, connecting, growing together, and holding space and boundaries for her children through parental leadership.

An experience that comes up a lot in Ashley's traditional family is around body boundaries, like her daughter not wanting to be hugged by an older relative: *"I'm her grandmother! Why won't she hug me?"* implying, of course, that the relative is owed the hug. As a sexual abuse survivor, Ashley is keenly aware of what happens when children override their bodily autonomy. Because Ashley values and understands the importance of body consent and how *any* unwanted physical contact impacts a child's esteem, Ashley held firm boundaries within her family so that they would respect her body boundaries.

But she struggled with feeling like she was overreacting. *"After all, wasn't it just a hug?"* Should she be making her daughter hug her grandmother as an act of respect? She ruminates, *"This isn't the sexual abuse I faced. It's just a relative asking for a hug."*

She describes the ongoing internal battle between her values (in this case: body autonomy) and a lifetime of conditioning (in this case: respect your elders). It's taken a tremendous amount of inner work to land on the idea of coherence. Ashley describes this concept of coherence as an integration and hierarchy of her values. She is clear that the value of 'body consent' supersedes the value of 'respect.' To arrive here, we must understand how our past influences our triggers and how it affects the values that guide our parenting. From a newfound awareness, we can choose how to respond in those moments with grounding, boundaries, and coherence.

✳

The first step toward Peaceful Parenting is becoming aware of, naming, and integrating how the experiences that we had as children influence the way we relate to others (including our kids) as adults.

Attachment theory describes three flavors of insecure attachment: ambivalent, disorganized, and avoidant. Notice what you recognize in yourself in the chart below without judging yourself or your parents (as much as possible). The value of this exercise is in recognition. It's not necessary to relive the past to gain perspective from our awareness.

This practice is more like watching a car chase in a movie than being in the car chase. We can recognize that we are watching the movie and not in the movie.

Similarly, we are looking at the past. We are not in the past. You are safe. You are reading a book that is lovingly inviting you to recognize some patterns that are not serving you or your children.

We do this as a way to pave a new path forward versus feeling blame, shame, remorse, or resentment about things in the past. They happened. We can't change that. Insight and awareness around these issues show us how we can improve our relationships with ourselves, our children, and our loved ones.

AVOIDANT ATTACHMENT

As a child, your primary caregiver:

- May have ignored you and your attempts to meet your needs for connection. They were not present in their bodies.
- May have struggled with vulnerability and avoided a close connection with you.
- Didn't share much about themselves and typically stayed quiet and nondescript.
- May have become angry at you often for small things and had limited capacity for feeling and/or witnessing emotions.
- May have expressed, verbally or nonverbally, that you were a burden or a "handful," perhaps having this belief about themselves.

As a parent, with yourself, you may:

- Feel numb to your feelings and your body.
- Struggle to connect to those closest to you or let someone close to you.
- Not remember your childhood.
- Dismiss your childhood: "yeah, I was mistreated, but now I'm fine!" This may manifest as a literal and logical way of making sense of your life without considering the more subtle nuances like emotion, connection, and relationships.
- Not taking time to self-reflect and be curious about your inner experiences.
- Want to run away, literally, when you are experiencing stress.
- Avoid conflict and sweep things under the rug.
- Not communicate your needs because you do not know what they are and assume they will not get met anyway. You just don't have many needs.
- You want to do better for your child but have

trouble connecting in meaningful ways.

- Live with a deep-seated fear of rejection.

As a parent with your child, you may:

- Sense a dismissive attachment with your child. Not able to truly connect and understand what they need.
- See your child as needy and feel resentful at times or suffocated about how much they depend on you.
- Want your child to be self-sufficient at an incredibly young age. (Even when a child is old enough to do things for themselves, they often still want their special person by their side!)
- Struggle to hold space for your child's feelings and think they are over dramatic.
- Deny vulnerability.

- Focus on hyper independence.
- Need a lot of space from your child and view your child as clingy.
- Tend to boost their self-image by ignoring/rejecting negative beliefs about themselves. AKA toxic positivity.
- Want your child to self-soothe at a young age. (Children need inter-soothing or "borrow their parent's calm" until around age 12!)
- Place extreme emphasis on science and material evidence, and feel that emotions are uncomfortable and inconvenient.

Your child: (Caveat: These manifestations could be from an insecure-avoidant attachment or other mental health/physical health diagnoses)

- Avoids connection with you. Would rather be alone.
- Seems withdrawn, spacey, and has trouble focusing or concentrating.

- Struggles with memory and may appear irresponsible.
- Struggles with emotional regulation, erupts and won't allow you to soothe them.

- Does not communicate how they feel or what they think. They may shut down or hide away from you rather than have a hard conversation.
- May struggle with empathy for siblings or others. *(P.S. the adult should know that the anterior insular cortex, which drives empathy, takes many years to develop fully. As a result, empathy should not always be expected. It begins to develop around age 9!)*

AMBIVALENT ATTACHMENT

As a child, your primary caregiver:

- May have given help when you did not need it and withheld help when you did.
- May have believed they needed to save you from your feelings with constant reassurance or distraction from upsets.
- Felt very insecure and afraid of their job as a parent. Constantly doubted themselves.
- Was not emotionally reliable; sometimes very present and warm, sometimes distant and cold.
- Experienced a lot of anxiety while tending to you, which you inevitably absorbed into your developing brain and nervous system as a child.
- May have expressed with body language and/or verbal cues that you were stupid, incompetent, unable to do anything right, or "will never learn!" Or, they may have had these unconscious beliefs about themselves, which radiated as unspoken and normalized truths within the family system.

As a parent, with yourself, you may:

- Experience an anxious disposition: *Feeling anxious about feeling anxious.*
- Get lost in worst-case scenarios more often than not.

- Feel emotionally unstable, go through a roller coaster of feelings quickly, and feel unable to find a sense of calm.
- Start projects and not follow through.
- Struggle with shame and beliefs of worthlessness.
- Swing between feeling confident and secure to lost and anxious.
- Have chronic self-doubt as a parent.
- Feel very strong self-blame and believe you are unworthy of love.
- Rely heavily on others because you *just can't do it!*
- Worry chronically about your child, how you're not *doing enough* or *failing them.*

As a parent with your child, you may:

- Sense a "preoccupied attachment" to your child. (Review this important concept in *The Power of Showing Up*, if necessary.)
- Have difficulty giving your child space when requested or allowing others to help; constantly worry that your child needs you.
- Worry about the child's well-being and obsess over illness or worst-case scenarios.
- Desire your child to be calm and regulated so that YOU can be calm and regulated.
- Not set limits or expectations, fearing your child will be mad at you.

Your child: *(Caveat: These manifestations could be from an insecure ambivalent attachment or other mental health/physical health diagnoses)*

- Struggles with anxiety.
- Is fearful of uncertainty.
- Struggles to self-regulate and has many episodes of emotional eruption each day.
- Struggles to connect with friends.
- Doesn't want to leave the house and wants to be with their caregiver at all times.
- Struggles with focus; experiences a mind that is constantly spinning.

DISORGANIZED ATTACHMENT

As a child, your primary caregiver:

- May have acted in ways that scared you, with no repair process in place after scary events.
- May have feared your feelings, especially your cries. Your emotions were *too much.*
- May have been emotionally distraught much of the time (whether outward presenting or something you sensed).
- Screamed chronically, used name-calling, threats, shame, and fear tactics to control the child's behavior.
- Swung between despondent and depressed and angry and erratic.

- Practiced authoritarian parenting and could not create a safe environment or protect you from harm.
- Used corporal punishment. (The intentional use of physical force to cause bodily pain or discomfort as a penalty for unacceptable behavior.) Corporal punishment includes any action that produces discomfort, such as spanking (even when done calmly), hitting, slapping, pinching, ear-pulling, jabbing, shoving, or choking).

As a parent with yourself, you may:

- Have difficulty staying focused and on task, feeling confused and "swirly" on the inside much of the time.
- Be unable to cope with stress and feel very disoriented about your thoughts/feelings.

- Experience a sense of not really existing. Like you're here, but you're not here.
- Have moments of physical aggression and violence.
- Go through very high highs and very low lows.

- Have an exceptionally low tolerance for loud noise or conflict between siblings.

- Feel very lost and alone deep down.

As a parent with your child, you may:

- Scream, hit, threaten with violence, or use derogatory language to get your children to obey. You may often feel out of control.
- Struggle with chronic reactivity and be unable to stand your child's big feelings.
- Take your child's behaviors and words very personally.
- Feel that any kind of feedback from your child is harsh criticism of you.

- Become angry easily and direct your anger onto your child, making your child fear you.
- Struggle to have any kind of connection with your child other than *command and obey.*
- Become enraged very easily, suddenly snapping nearly every day. Feelings of total hate and rage for your child/ren, that seemingly come from nowhere!

Your child: (*Caveat: These manifestations could be from an insecure disorganized attachment or other mental health/physical health diagnoses*)

- May be consistently eruptive and easily become angry and seem to snap over little things.
- May not trust authority figures and not like to listen to anyone in a power-over position.
- May use violence and aggression to meet their

needs for connection, to be seen, and to be heard.
- Does not compromise and talks back. Their brain has already wired itself to defend against anything a parent/authority says to them.
- Uses hate speech to parents or siblings and seems defiant or out of control.

- May want you suddenly, then reject you right away.
- Seems very fearful and suspicious.
- Struggles with huge outbursts of rage and will not receive any support from any caregiver. They believe that adults are dangerous and not to be trusted.
- Oscillates between being unreachable and shut down and being out of control and aggressive

*Note: If you notice any of these tendencies in your child, it is OKAY. We understand that reading this may bring up feelings of overwhelm, fear, shame, remorse, anger, and many more. These feelings make complete sense!

If you and/or your child live with an avoidant, insecure, or ambivalent attachment system—this is not bad or wrong. It just is. You are here to learn how to support your child to feel safer, more secure, and more self-connected! There is always hope.

❋

One of the most powerful ways to bring cohesiveness from our past into our future is to recognize the powerful qualities of resilience that come from having challenging experiences. Things that create darkness can also create light if we are willing to allow it!

The path to allowing our light to shine brightly is acknowledging the gifts we acquired through our life's more challenging experiences.

About ten years ago, I was standing in my kitchen, reading a blog post I'd just written about the way my stepmother treated my half-brother and me. He was regularly locked in the bathroom for an hour at a time. She put tabasco and soap in his mouth (yes, at the same time) when he talked back. One summer, when I was fifteen and most likely carrying the extra padding that often comes with puberty, she told me I was fat and only let me eat plain broiled salmon and white rice for dinner every night for six weeks! I didn't eat salmon again for twenty years.

Anyway, I was standing at the counter, reading the blog, and it hit me like a punch in the gut. This was abuse. My brother and I suffered emotional and, in his case, physical abuse. I was an abused child. What she did was beyond defense.

It had never occurred to me before. I would just tell myself she was mean. I didn't want to be around her. When she and my dad divorced, I felt relieved. Four years ago, my kids met her at my brother's wedding; their intuition was incredible.

"Mom, why does that lady feel so mean?"

But here's the powerful truth: Had that not happened to my brother and me, or if it had happened in a different context (if she were my birth mother, I wouldn't have the perspective of how my mother parented me—not perfectly—but certainly not violently) none of us would be here reading this book.

There would be no Jai Institute for Parenting. We wouldn't have reached the thousands upon thousands of families we've touched through this work. What happened to my brother and me was awful. What happened to my brother and me had a purpose.

Let me show you the amazing qualities of each insecure attachment style so that you can find the beauty that emerged from your childhood challenges. Each of the attachment styles comes with attachment superpowers.

Find yours. Celebrate them. And see if you can find gratitude for the fire you had to walk through to integrate these powerful human attributes.

THE SUPERPOWERS OF THE INSECURE ATTACHMENT STYLES

Let's stop telling ourselves the story that because we have some inse-cure areas to work on, there's anything wrong with us. Not only is there nothing wrong with you, but there's so much right. Each of the inse-cure attachment styles comes with some superpowers. These are likely attributes that you are recognized for and that (I hope!) you love about yourself. See where you recognize yourself below.

As a parent living with more moments of AVOIDANCE than security, your strengths may be:

- You may give your child a lot of space and freedom. You don't struggle with hovering or always needing to be involved in what they are doing.
- You are independent and can teach your children how to do things on their own in a way that truly serves them.
- You may have an easier time respecting your child's boundaries because you know how important it is for people to give you the space you need.
- You may easily access the positive side to difficult situations, which can serve your child to have an ability to look at the glass as half full.
- You may feel quite confident as a parent and don't spend much time in self-doubt.

As a parent living with more moments of AMBIVALENCE than secu-rity, your strengths may be:

- Your heart is HUGE! You care deeply and strongly.
- You are constantly learning and trying to grow, evolve, and heal.
- When you can, you may thrive at tuning into your child's feel-ings and needs.

- Parenting is your priority, and you will make life changes necessary for your children to be in the center.
- You are usually caring and considerate of how your actions will impact your child and are willing to take responsibility for your actions.

As a parent living with more moments of DISORGANIZATION and disequilibrium than security, your strengths may be:

- You seek connection with your child when able.
- You care a lot about your relationship with your child and can access moments of genuine desire to improve and be a safe harbor for your child.
- You can experience both independence as a parent and immersion in parenting.
- You love deeply.
- When you can access a positive state of mind, gratitude and appreciation can overwhelm you with good feelings.
- You are very creative and flexible—able to see all sides of a situation when in a calm state.
- You are usually very compassionate for animals or other people who experience suffering.

THE GREAT LETTING-GO OF OUR PAST

Laura grew up in a household where cleanliness and order reigned. To Laura's mother, nothing was more important than keeping an immaculate house. Laura discovered as a child that she simply wasn't built that way and could not live up to her mother's impeccable standards.

Once she became a mother, Laura didn't anticipate how this would manifest in her own home until one day, she sat down to play with her son and noticed dirt on one spot of the carpet as she sat down to play the game. She got up to vacuum it, and before she knew it, she had vacuumed the entire house while her son waited and eventually gave up.

She had become her mother.

Then her mom announced a visit. Fearing judgment, Laura scheduled a housecleaner to come the morning of her mother's arrival. Everything would be perfect, so there would be nothing to judge!

Her mother arrived later that day. "Your kitchen is filthy," her mother announced.

Laura looked around. "What exactly are you looking at?"

She pointed up. "The top of the ceiling fan."

Crushed, Laura left the room to cry but then returned. "Mom, I know this is a wound for you. And I love you, but I can't help you." They cried together.

Laura found the compassion to see her mother as the product of *her* upbringing, another wounded person doing her best with what she had. And thus began a healing journey for both of them.

We justify our parents' actions through self-blame (inappropriately taking responsibility for their choices) as a path to maintain the relationship. As children, this is the most efficient way for our developing minds to try to make sense of our world. Accepting ourselves as the problem is easier than seeing our parents as the problem. We defend the undefendable to maintain our love (and sense of safety).

Many of us have been sold a story of forgiveness that says we must accept or excuse unacceptable behavior as part of the process. This implies that forgiveness revolves around the other person or people in the story. It's not about them. Forgiveness is for you. It's about how you interpret your experiences and how heavy or light they feel in your soul. Forgiveness does not mean downplaying the impact people's actions had on you. It is the recognition that anger and resentment make the experiences that hurt us *more* painful. Forgiveness is about freeing yourself from this additional layer of pain so you can define a new future for yourself and your family.

As this quote from Buddha reminds us, *"Holding on to anger is like grasping a hot coal with the intention of throwing it at someone else; you are the one who gets burned."*

Forgiveness is a process we engage in for ourselves and our children. We cannot show up as our whole selves, present, available, and ready to show unconditional love when we continue to carry our caregivers' past transgressions like emotional cinder blocks.

Forgiveness begins with a decision. We can make the empowered choice to release ourselves from the anger we feel over the choices and actions of others. Emotional healing is a journey of letting go, gently revisiting the past with the perspective of who you are as an adult.

Please know that most of us require support to do the courageous work of acknowledging what happened to us and how what happened to us has defined us.

> *"We are not responsible for what happened to us.*
> *We are responsible for how we choose to move*
> *forward despite what happened to us."*

As a coach, one of my favorite concepts I share with my clients is "putting down the bag of rocks." A lot of us have already done a lot of therapy. We've tried to heal and forgive. We lament the past we did not have. The stories we tell about the people, events, and experiences that were wrong, painful, unfair, and traumatic are the rocks. So much freedom comes from realizing that you can just put them down. Let them go. Instead of focusing your attention on what didn't serve your past, focus your attention on what will serve your future. Release what no longer serves you.

You are here to create a new operating system for your family. The old operating system is obsolete. It was the normal system for a long time. We are leaving it behind and creating a new and better future for ourselves, our kids, and even their future kids!

By looking at our past from a new perspective, we access greater empathy. We can extend this to our parents who lacked the skills, resources, or knowledge to do things differently. This does not negate the effects their choices and actions had on us. This loosens our grip on righteousness, so we free ourselves of resentment and anger. This allows us to access more energy for connection, joy, and peace.

A note: We have all behaved in ways that have hurt others. This doesn't make it o.k. But it is human. Remember, forgiveness is for you.

Empathy opens a new space in our stories and experiences. It gives us a new perspective. It loosens the grip of our one-sided truth. Naturally, in experiences of abuse, there are limits to the places we can go. Allow those limits to stay in place, as needed, for your mental health. There is no need to go further than feels safe.

One of the best ways to do this is to come to peace with the idea that two seemingly contradictory ideas can be true simultaneously. Holding two truths allows you to celebrate your parents' strengths, challenges, and experiences while also acknowledging the impact of their actions, words, and deeds on your sense of self-worth and esteem.

Example: "My mother loved me. It wasn't right that she left me alone so much."

As you hold these dichotomies in your awareness, you'll gain access to a deeper and more honest understanding of your past. Your reactivity will naturally diminish. Space will be created for you to intentionally create the new family system that will carry you and your children into a more peaceful future... a future rooted in Secure Attachment:

SECURE ATTACHMENT:

As a child, especially in your first few years of life, your primary caregiver:

- Was self-connected and felt trusted to be your caretaker.
- Mirrored your facial expressions.
- Gave you verbal empathy like: "You feel a bit down today?" or "Do you need a hand? I am wondering if you need support with that?"
- Offered you grounded care: "Come here, hon, I've got a hug for you."
- Understood your behaviors while trying to meet your needs and was not threatened or afraid of the behaviors.
- Encouraged you to discuss your feelings, hopes, dreams, and wishes, and was able to hold space for you and actively listen, versus fix, problem-solve, or shut down.

- Apologized to you when they made a mistake without being self-deprecating.
- Soothed you whenever you needed it, day or night.
- Met their own needs and was proactive in requesting support.
- Guessed what you were thinking to understand your actions better.
- Communicated with you to understand and connect instead of needing to be right or make a point.
- Was not perfect! They modeled self-compassion and an understanding that striving for perfection was impossible.

As a parent with yourself, you may find that more often than not:

- You pay attention to your body and what it communicates to you.
- You pay attention to your feelings and embrace all feelings as "communicators with messages."
- You remember your childhood with compassion and understanding. You have made a coherent narrative.
- You can forgive yourself easily when you make a mistake and take accountability to ensure it does not happen again.
- You are actively engaged in friendships and community and understand this as a CORE component of health and well-being; you can regulate emotionally.
- You know what you need and believe you're inherently worthy of meeting those needs.
- You feel confident in your communication and have a strong window of tolerance when negotiating contrasting needs/wants/desires.
- You believe your child is unique and valuable and worthy of prioritizing.

As a parent with your child:

- You feel confident providing a haven and a secure base for your child.
- You can see beneath the child's behavior into their feelings and needs.
- You approach your child with grounded awareness when they seek closeness and connection.
- You can understand and differentiate between the experiences, thoughts, and feelings of yourself and your child.
- you can remain grounded and connected to joy if your child is upset or grumpy.
- You can model regulation and soothe your child (*no matter their age!*) when needed.
- You can communicate feelings and needs directly without

passive-aggressiveness, making your child guess what is going on or giving the child the silent treatment.

- You can prioritize emotional, physical, psychological, and spiritual bonds with children despite criticism from others.
- You can actively decondition your parenting from harsh punishments, covert punishments, or power-over or under-parenting tactics.

Your child:

- Believes that they are worthy of love.
- Accepts the parent's bid for connection.
- Can verbalize boundaries in a clear way (7 and older). "Mom, please shut my door. I want space." *Note—when the child is stressed at any age, clear communication may significantly decrease!*
- Is more willing to work as a team and has empathy for actions (7 and older).
- Can regulate their emotions and self-soothe some of the time, knowing that even adults need co-regulation, rather than self-regulation, some of the time (7 and older).
- Welcomes the parent's longing to support the child to be soothed (especially infant-7).
- Is drawn to friendship circles that enhance their self-esteem and mirror a healthy lifestyle (7-teens).
- Can focus on academics and maintain concentration (7 and older). *Even children with a secure attachment may struggle with diagnoses such as ADD and ADHD. Being securely attached can help reduce the symptoms of both of these neurological experiences.*
- Is independent, with a healthy relationship, self-agency, and self-awareness (12 and older).
- Believes that life is good, that they are worthy, and that no matter the difficulties, they will find a way to work through them.
- If living with neurodiversity or a mental and/or physical illness, they can be more capable of accessing

self-acceptance and trust within their life experience.

- Is not perfect and is at peace with this.

> Chapter Bonus: Download the supplemental guide and journaling prompts for Making Peace with Your Parenting Past at www.jaiinstituteforparenting.com/book-resources

MYLES, AGE 17

What do you know about the way I was parented?

I know you were alone a lot and didn't have a lot of supervision or support. And I know that you had a pretty wild streak as a teenager because of it.

That's definitely true! How do you think that's affected how I parent you and your sister?

I think you care a lot about being a really good mom. And that you try to balance being our mom while still giving us the freedom to make our own choices and solve our own problems.

Can you share an example of that?

Myles: Hmmm…. Well, one I can think of right now is that you don't get over-involved in our grades and homework. When I had a grade that I wasn't happy with last semester, you asked me, "What do you choose to do about it?" That's a question you ask us a lot. So then I know you'll help me brainstorm solutions, but you've learned not to try to fix it for me.

What happens when I try to fix it? Because I've definitely crossed that line a few times?

(Both laugh.)

I feel like it shuts me down to your advice. It makes me feel like you don't think I'm smart enough to figure it out myself. It makes me feel like you don't trust me.

How do you think your life would be different if I didn't learn to parent you and Charlotte differently than the way I was parented?

I mean, there have been times in my life when you've been my best friend... my only friend, really. And I don't know how I would have gotten through those if we didn't have the kind of relationship that we have. The fact that we always have open lines of communication, even when things go wrong or are really hard. I don't know what would have happened if we didn't have that. I think I'd be really angry and bitter.

CHAPTER FOUR

The Great Surrender

A client of Jenny's contacted her to support her grown son, who had gone on sixty interviews without being offered a job. His parents were desperate to get him launched and out of their house. They hoped that Jenny's background in human resources and her skills as a parenting coach could help him "get it together."

This was not a family that was short on resources or connections. Dad was a successful investment banker in New York, they owned multiple homes, and their kids all went to the best schools. They were worried about their son's inability to land a job after graduating with honors from Boston College. He'd been "the perfect kid."

Jenny agreed to sit down with him to try and shed some light on what was going wrong. She thought that some mock interviews would help him improve his skills.

She began by asking him, "What accomplishments have you achieved that make you feel proud?" His reply revealed everything Jenny needed to know.

He said he was the captain of the hockey team because his parents wanted him to be. He was an All-American football player for the same reason. He went to the same college as his dad. He made *them* proud.

With further inquiry, Jenny realized this young man didn't know who he was beyond what his parents wanted for him. He didn't know what he had done in his life that authentically came from his interests or passions. He had no inner locus of confidence, experience, or independence. From the get-go, he'd been protected, molded, and shaped into who his parents wanted him to be. At twenty-two years old, he had no idea who he was or what he stood for. He didn't know what he wanted to do, be, or have. He was lost, despite being given every privilege.

THE MOTHER OF ALL PROJECTION

As we've stated, traditional parenting tells us that it is a primary responsibility to keep our children safe. And, of course, children's safety *is* paramount. However, what deserves exploration, is what we define as safety.

Because we also cause harm if we surround our kids with proverbial bubble wrap, protecting them, wanting for them, and needing them to show up:

- Happy
- Excited
- Enthusiastic
- Motivated
- Responsible
- Well-behaved

- Appreciative
- (should I go on?)

All. Of. The. Time.

When we reject any aspect of our child's human experience, they hear that there is a part of them that is not wanted, lovable, or acceptable.

If we get really honest about the expectations of traditional parenting, what we discover is that it is *all about the feelings and needs of the parent*. Parents want their children to be less triggering. We try to control their behavior, actions, and choices in the name of our sanity. We want them to be the star athlete or student to bolster our sense of worthiness and accomplishment.

We make our fears their fears.

We make our dreams their dreams.

We don't want them to experience the hardships we experienced, so we micromanage their lives and inadvertently keep them from their own.

We make our feelings their responsibility.

Basically, we project the bleep all over them.

And . . . They don't like it.

I don't know about you, but when anyone tries to control me, I feel tightness in my chest. My nervous system immediately activates dysregulation, and I want to run (or fight—depending on who is doing the controlling).

It's not any different for our kids. Control can look like many things. It's easy to look out into the world and see control at work. We can see its negative impact. Jenny shared her experience with her controlling father in our gatherings to write this book.

Jenny was nineteen and in her senior year of college when she fell in love with a black man. Jenny is white. The two had been dating for about a year when Jenny's dad informed her that he would cut her off from his financial support if she didn't end the relationship. She was financially dependent on her father. He was paying for college, her apartment, and her car. Jenny loved her boyfriend, and she was, therefore, unwilling to accept her dad's racist and unjust ultimatum. She said, "I'll be damned if I was going to give in because of who I fell in love with." She told her father that she would not submit to his request. Shortly after, Jenny's dad showed up, took her car, and told her she was cut off. Jenny's mother had died four months earlier, so she was alone in the world.

Jenny became homeless as a result of losing her father's support. She stole vegetables and fruit from strangers' gardens and drove up her credit card balances, just trying to survive.

Years later, when her dad was dying, he told her how proud he was of her for sticking to her convictions all those years earlier.

When Jenny told us this story, she described feeling that her father had given her an incredible gift. She even credited the experience for making her a stronger and more resilient woman. She shied away from talking about the trauma that she experienced.

We have been led to believe that these moments of power-over parenting make us better people. We believe this in part because it protects us from acknowledging the pain our parents caused.

It's not about blaming our parents. It's about acknowledging the truth of what happened. That some (or lots) of what happened wasn't right. If we fail to face the truth of the pain they caused us and don't take steps to reconcile our hurt, we risk projecting our wounding onto our children.

Jenny knows that even in his extreme and intolerant choice, her dad genuinely believed he was doing the right thing. She feels that her father believed that by having an interracial relationship, Jenny would have a difficult life. He believed that taking an extreme stance was responsible. But that didn't mean it was right.

Jenny was able to heal from the experience, acknowledge the gifts and move on, both in her relationship with her dad and in her life. Sadly, this isn't always how the story ends. This could just as easily have been a story that ended with a lifetime of struggle, addiction, and homelessness.

We must stop glorifying resilience as a justification for treating children harshly. Children raised in loving, supportive, nurturing environments are also very resilient. We don't need to treat children harshly to prepare them for the world.

Our children will be hurt physically, emotionally, and spiritually. They will have broken hearts and broken arms. They will get fired from a job, and they won't get into their first choice of colleges. They will fail.

Our work here is to minimize the *unnecessary* pain caused by normal, traditional parenting. Let's demolish the thought that we need to "toughen up our kids" to prepare them for the "real world." And on the other side of the equation, if we protect them from the "real world," we also cause them harm. So then, what can we do?

Ok, so take a deep breath with me and let this sink in:

If we shelter our kids from experiencing pain, failure, and the natural consequences of their immature decisions while they are in the safe nest of our loving hearts and homes, how, in the name of all that is, will they learn to handle challenges when they leave?

If we make every decision for them, how can they be expected to know how to make decisions for themselves when the time comes?

Ashley shared a story of coaching a ten-year-old girl whose parents were worried about her. She was shy and didn't have a lot of self-confidence. Her mom was apprehensive about how her friends were treating her.

Ashley was teaching this young girl about how habits get formed through neural pathways in the brain, and she mentioned that "it's kind of like learning to brush your teeth when you're small! Now you probably don't even think about it!"

"I don't brush my teeth," responded the girl.

"What do you mean?" asked Ashley.

"My mom brushes my teeth for me. She says I don't do a good enough job."

Of course, Ashley was surprised by what she'd just learned. "What about other ways you take care of yourself? How about washing your hair?"

"No," she said, "my mom washes my hair, too."

Later that day, Ashley had a brave conversation with the mom. "If you could just put yourself in your daughter's shoes for a moment, what message do you think she's getting from you?" The mom paused. You could tell she was feeling the pain of her recognition.

She realized that fear was driving her parenting.

"That she's not good enough."

We are going to have to let go someday. It's best to start practicing now.

Our child's life is not ours to live. It is their life. (And their teeth! And hair! And stuff!)

Peaceful Parenting aims to equip our children to handle all aspects of their lives (positive and challenging), with a sense of self, values, and morals illuminating their way.

This means that the modern parenting paradigm invites us to teach, mentor, and guide our children while simultaneously surrendering control as they become more independent and mature.

Let's examine this through the lens of what traditional parenting tells us to expect from our kids:

- The tantruming twos.
- Three-nagers (meaning our three-year-olds are making petulant demands).
- The frightening fours.
- Pre-teen drama.
- Teenage rebellion.

All these experiences result from a rejection of control and uninformed or unrealistic expectations of children. If it's absolutely normal for a two-year-old brain to be flooded with hormones that make them extra sensitive, then why are we perpetuating the idea that the toddler needs to learn to control themselves? A teenager's brain is reorganizing every single synapse. Of course, they are going to forget to take out the trash. They've lost access to big parts of their brain. It has nothing to do with their love or respect for their parents. And yet we shame, criticize, and diminish them and then wonder why they're so cranky.

When we admonish our kids for doing something they didn't do on purpose, don't have the brain wiring yet to do, or make them wrong for simply being human, it's no wonder they act out, reject us, and withdraw to their rooms.

These experiences are not necessary nor prescribed. They are all outcomes of the rejection our child very understandably feels when we deny their experience, feelings, wants, or needs.

Yes, we want to raise our children well. But this does not mean denying their human rights of expression, feelings, and choices.

Maria Montessori says to follow the child. When we do, our children will lead us to magical places. We must learn to allow them to lead.

"BUT . . . BUT . . . BUT . . . How will they learn to behave?"

We will teach them. With love, care, attention, and presence. We will teach them with our actions and words. We will model the behavior we aspire for them to emulate. We will allow them to fall, and be there when they come home with bloody knees, to soothe their hurts, without denying them or blaming and shaming them for their "mistakes."

. . . Pretty much every two-year-old stops tantruming.

. . . Pretty much every four-year-old becomes the sweetest nine-year-old.

. . . Pretty much every teenager becomes a functional adult.

Maybe we can give them the space to grow by lovingly, tenderly, and bravely getting the heck out of their way.

Transformation happens when we provide our presence, guidance, listening, love, and affection as they travel through their journey to adulthood.

My son never quite fit in socially in our local schools. He feels things deeply and is used to being able to express and share his feelings. This never went over very well in the public high school cafeteria.

But he spent the first semester of his junior year of high school at a school in Vermont. And "found his people." He called after the first week and shared, "Mom! I can make friends! Everyone likes me here! It's not me. It's the situation!"

Then, he met a girl.

The response was pretty standard as I shared this happy outcome with close friends and family. "But she lives so far away! He's going to have his heart broken."

"Yes," was my standard reply. Of course, he's going to get his heart broken. And while my mama's heart aches with this knowledge, I know how vital it will be for him to experience heartbreak to deepen his capacity for love.

We can teach our children to fear what life has to offer, or we can teach them to handle it. Their heartbreaks, failures, and the natural consequences of the decisions that they are allowed to make are as important to their human evolution as learning to chew with their mouths closed.

Would you rather have your child grow up afraid of the world and the unknowns or march bravely into the unknown with a full sense of self-worth and confidence? I opt for the latter.

Would you rather have a child who fits in or a child who stands out? Not by their accomplishments or achievements, but because they know who they are, what they care about, what they will tolerate and what they won't.

Another poignant conversation with my son Myles: That year, when he struggled to fit into public high school, he felt so isolated and alone. He was lamenting the behavior of his peers in the lunchroom. A group of boys had been throwing food and leering at girls that day. He picked up his tray and moved to another table to sit by himself. Wanting him to have a better experience, I asked him, "Do you want to start acting like the other kids act? Just in the name of being able to have friends?"

His answer was immediate and unequivocal: "No," he stated firmly, "I will not pretend to be someone I'm not. I'm not interested in acting that way nor being friends with people who do."

"O.K., son. O.K.!"

"I guess I didn't raise you to fit in. I raised you to think. And lead. That's probably making your life harder right now, but I trust it will serve you well in the long run."

Children are born curious and wise. They are born with natural inclinations, talents, and dreams. We get to learn to trust them by slowly letting go of control. When we trust them, we receive the greatest gift. They trust us back. More importantly, they learn they can also trust themselves.

We won't be with our children forever. One day, we will age and leave. Our children will grow up, leave home, and carve out their future.

Allowing opportunities for your child to develop into their person is the best gift we can ever give them.

※

Becoming aware of the subtle ways in which we are exerting control over our children is brave and introspective work. A powerful indicator is available to us in our bodies. We come with an inner warning system that we can learn to recognize. It's the way you feel when there is danger.

Remember a time when perhaps your child ran into a crosswalk without looking both ways or was running toward a swimming pool before they knew how to swim. Maybe they fell and banged their head—hard—and you noticed the first signs of a concussion.

Your entire nervous system lit up. You sprang into action. Perhaps you felt your face get hot or extreme tightness in your chest. Maybe (probably!) you yelled, "STOP!"

Maybe your knees buckled, or you felt nauseous.

These are all very normal reactions in the face of genuine danger, and in these circumstances, it is an excellent thing that our brains initiate a fight, flight, or freeze response.

This response is initiated by the amygdala of the brain, which sends a distress signal to the hypothalamus to flood the body with cortisol and adrenaline stress hormones.

This happens unconsciously and quickly. After the reaction initiates, the higher levels of the brain, namely the prefrontal cortex, come online and create a rational narrative for the reaction. So rational thought doesn't drive our reactivity. *Rational thought justifies our reactivity.*

Bear with me here. I promise this will all come together because here's the kicker: The amygdala cannot distinguish between a real or a perceived threat.

Now time for another embarrassing story from the founder of a parenting institute:

I was a dancer growing up, and when I was about eleven, my teacher told me that my dream of a future as a ballerina was over because my hips were growing in the wrong direction. I kept dancing, finding love for modern dance, but I received the message: If you want to succeed in life, you'd better stay thin.

A few months into COVID, my fourteen-year-old daughter came downstairs in a sports bra one morning. It was as if she went upstairs in March with one body and came downstairs in May with another. I remember feeling shocked seeing her tummy and arms, and chest. I started to make "helpful" comments about her food choices and suggested that we watch sugar documentaries together. (I know, awful. AWFUL.)

The more "helpful" I tried to be, the more she withdrew to her room. The more sullen she became. And the more she turned to food for comfort.

I felt righteous in my mothering because my entire nervous system screamed danger, DANGER!

After some processing with my therapist and some dear friends who were willing to call me out, I found that my entire being was operating from a below-the-surface belief that fat is not safe. But when I really examined this, it was complete and utter ridiculousness. I have many friends who live in bigger bodies who are smart, sexy, funny, loving, and happy.

I perceived danger. There was none. And my perception and desire to control my daughter's body took a serious toll on my daughter's sense of self-worth and our relationship.

I was blind to what was happening. It felt right! It felt real! It felt scary!

And it was a lie.

(It took almost a year, and lots of gentle conversations and me being very honest with my daughter about what happened in order to repair and mend, which we will talk about later in this book. The good news? There's nothing broken that can't be fixed.)

We try to control our kids because we are scared of what will happen if we don't.

And so the opportunity is to start to get curious about your own "There's DANGER!" response by asking, "Is there real danger? Or is this about me?"

Is it true that if your child doesn't want to play a sport anymore, they are lazy?

Is it true that they don't respect you if they don't clean their room? And what does respecting you even mean? That they always do what you say when you say it? And also, do you *really* want a kid who always complies with the authority figure in the room?

The thing that you are sure they need to do? Do they? Need to? And why?

As we learn to regulate our own nervous system, we need less from our children. We don't need them to stay quiet, so we don't feel stressed. As we learn to find our own sense of purpose and creativity, we don't need to use their achievements to signify our worth. We care less about other people's thoughts and stop using our children as a shield against our insecurities. As we learn to heal our childhood wounds and recognize the triggers that affect our parenting, we stop needing to be overprotective around things that aren't present or likely.

As a survivor of early sexual trauma, Lisa was hypervigilant about her daughter's physical safety. She was sure that if her daughter posted pictures of herself on Instagram that pedophiles would find out where they lived. This fear loomed so powerfully in Lisa's system that she became what her daughter's friends called the "Insta-police," calling their mothers when she perceived that they were putting themselves at risk on social media.

Her daughter was mortified. You know what else? Her daughter was safe. She'd always been safe. There aren't actually pedophiles on every corner. And while we can have compassion for Lisa's fears, we can also see how they were destroying her relationship with her child.

So here's the ultimate leap of faith: When we give our kids room to breathe and have more and more autonomy over their lives… When we save our parenting moments for the things that matter and let almost everything else go, we save our future relationship with our child.

Only you can decide what matters to your family, guided by your values, beliefs, and morals. And still, your child is not you. It's important to hear this because otherwise, we perpetuate the harm that comes with the idea that our children need to keep up appearances so that we feel better. They don't owe us this. They don't owe us much of anything. We have the responsibility as their parents. We owe them.

There will come a time when they can do whatever they want, whether we control their lives for them until they grow up or not.

Let's tell the truth: The more we try to control them, the more they will resist, avoid, resent, rage, and rebel against us. Traditional parenting says: Control the child. Be their guardian. They are a reflection of you.

Peaceful Parenting says: Trust the child. Be their guide. They are their own person.

Learn to recognize and take responsibility for where that control has been a part of your approach, knowing you can only do better when you know better. If you are heavy with any feelings of guilt, regret, or shame at this moment, it's ok. Breathe.

Remember, there's nothing broken that can't be fixed. Nothing. It's never too late. Guilt is a powerful emotion that guides us toward more integrity, cohesiveness, and wisdom.

Keep reading. We have so much hope to share with you.

ANDREW, AGE 5

What do you like the best about the way mommy and daddy treat you?

Um, gimme hugs and kisses.

Have you ever gotten in trouble for doing something wrong?

Sometimes?

Can you think of what happened?

I sometimes punch Nina. She gets mad, and dad gets really mad. And when I hurt and I say, stupid mom, stupid mom, mom. Mom's the stupidest. She gets mad.

Yeah. So if you do something with your hands or if you say some mean words, then people around you get mad. Is that what happens?

Yeah.

Hey, how do you feel when you see that Nina gets mad when you hit her or that mommy feels mad? If you say stupid, mommy, how do you feel?

Mad.

But do you get punished?

I get grounded.

Really? What does it mean to be "grounded"?

It means that mommy and I go sit in my room together until I feel calmer.

CHAPTER FIVE

Let's Change the World by Changing the Way We Parent

M argaret and Gerry knew that they wanted to parent their children differently than they were parented. Here's the thing: They had this revelation in 1978 before Peaceful Parenting was a thing. They wanted to be intentional about creating a family environment in which their three boys felt encouraged, nurtured, supported, and became kind, thoughtful, contributing members of the world. Even though it was the 1970s and the power-over parenting model was completely the norm, they knew it wasn't the right path for them.

Margaret was a home economics graduate who expressed her extensive talents in creating a warm, welcoming, and endlessly adventurous home. Her husband Gerry studied agriculture and took over the family farm. Together they had three children over eight years. To do things differently, they joined a group of parents who were exploring Alfred Adler's belief in what he called a democratic parenting style. This approach radically viewed children as equal, integrated family members who were loved and accepted for their uniqueness. Children parented in this way were offered opportunities to try new things, make mistakes and develop their capacities in the world with their parents' loving support. They were encouraged to take on experiences without fear of failure, knowing they were loved and accepted. They felt natural consequences were built-in behavioral teachers.

Margaret and Gerry's children are adults now. Here's what they say they experienced because their parents were willing to abandon the ideals of 'normal' parenting: In their home growing up, there was rarely a raised voice, and they were never threatened or grounded the way their friends were. Conversations with Margaret and Gerry never felt like lectures. They expressed their values to their sons and created an environment of connection and clarity around those expectations.

If the boys behaved in destructive ways, like when one of the brothers and their cousin decided to smash some of the barn windows just for fun, they were simply required to replace the glass they had broken. They recall that their parents didn't react with anger. One of their sons says he remembers witnessing a friend being disciplined and yelled at by their parents and feeling that the parents seemed out of control and even dangerous to him.

Margaret and Gerry were gentle and encouraging toward their sons and were always enthusiastic about their boys' efforts, regardless of the outcome. Each describes feeling free to try new things as children and throughout their lives. There was a lot of space for curiosity and taking risks and no emphasis on achievement over enjoyment.

All three of their sons are now fathers themselves. They each have gentle demeanors and approach their parenting in a way that is loving, connected, and supportive of their children. They aren't controlling or concerned with how their children are judged by others, as long as they are happy, kind, and doing their best. Margaret and Gerry are the kind of grandparents you mostly see in movies. They are fun and engaged and play endlessly with their grandchildren. They bake and build and dress up in costumes. They create a wonderful environment for children to feel loved.

❋

For generations, we have told kids, implicitly and explicitly, that children are the problem and that they need to be different so that they stop being the problem that is the thorn in their parent's side. In the name of our sanity, we use our power to control their behavior.

It is a new age where we can recognize that no human being has the right to control another person. But can we embrace this as parents?

Trying to be better at something that doesn't actually create the desired outcome is kind of crazy. It's like dieting. We know it doesn't work, and yet how many people all over the world, at this very moment, are trying to be better dieters?

Traditional parenting insists that the parent has *authority* over the child. Sure, the parent has a *responsibility* to the child. Still, if we embrace authority as a guiding principle, we don't give children a chance to develop the inner authority and locus of control that will allow them to thrive as adults. It also gives parents a lot of leeway to excuse authoritarian (power-over) behaviors in the guise of authoritative parenting. We aren't the dictators of our family; we are leaders. And effective leaders inspire rather than demand.

Through this lens, we can see that control can't be the answer. Doing it better doesn't yield better results.

The four traditional parenting models—authoritarian, authoritative, permissive, and neglectful—are modeled on two axes. Responsiveness and demandingness. So, as an example, if a parent is highly demanding and highly responsive, they would fall into the authoritative quadrant.

But this model is missing something vital—children's and parents' emotions, feelings, and needs.

There is inflexibility in the traditional model when modern parenting is better served with flexibility. The idea that we should always be highly responsive and demanding puts so much pressure on parents and kids. There are times when we have to be highly responsive and demanding. When our child is in physical danger, it is not the time to explore inner emotions. Of course, we must exert our authority in those moments and situations. And there are times when we need to tend to our fears and allow our children a very long leash, taking a more passive stance, giving them space to feel their limits and freedom (when they get their driver's license, for example).

The revolution we invite in these pages is to take our rightful position as the adult in the room. As adults, we are responsible for our children's physical and emotional safety and well-being. We are also responsible for giving them more and more responsibility and the skills, tools, and inner compass to fend for themselves as they grow and mature. As we become attuned and aware, we can be far more flexible in our role as a parent.

One of the myths we face in our work is that all children need to be parented differently. That belief is true when controlling behavior is the guiding principle of parenting. Different children respond differently to various tools of manipulation. One child may respond to rewards, while another may respond to punishments. Neuro-diverse children have different needs from their parents to meet behavioral goals.

Everything changes when we shift the goalpost from behavior to guidance and leadership. Remember the Core Human Needs we visited in Chapter One! These needs are universal. So let's revisit them here:

Safety: Our physiological needs for shelter, food, water, physical safety, rest, and emotional well-being.

Variety: The need for excitement, unique experiences, and access to new information and change.

Validation: The desire to be seen, understood, and appreciated by others.

Significance: The need to know that we matter and are important to others.

Connection: The need to know that we can give and receive love and feel that we belong to a community.

Autonomy: The need to own the choices and decisions that we make for ourselves.

Growth: The desire to do better, learn more and gain expertise in the areas of life that matter most to us.

Contribution: The need to be of service to others and make the world a better place.

When we give others what they need, they become our collaborators in meeting our needs, even when they are three! Our role as our child's parent is to work together with our children to create a family system where everyone's needs are met. We will delve into this further in Chapter Seven.

Lina is Singaporean-Chinese. Her culture is known for "Tiger Parenting," a term first used by Yale Law School professor Amy Chua to describe her parenting style in her 2011 memoir, *Battle Hymn of the Tiger Mother*. Lina describes the enormous pressure she felt to push and mold her child into the perfect reflection of her culture's expectations. As a child, she was constantly compared to her siblings, cousins, and peers. The playground pressure was real, and she describes the simultaneous anxiety and hyper-alert state of the other moms at the playground, coupled with their constant need to affirm their kids' achievements, good behavior, and superiority.

Lina shares how much she used to feel like a failure when her child behaved outside of these expectations disguised as cultural norms.

She alternatively experienced moments of rejection when her child told her, "no," thinking to herself, "I didn't get to say 'no' to my parents when I was a child. What is wrong with me is that I have a kid who doesn't seem to understand that he's supposed to do what I say!"

She felt depressed, defeated, and overwhelmed. The pressure she was putting on herself was taking a toll. Her confidence as a parent deteriorated. Her mind was full of critical thoughts, supposed to's, and should-haves. There was very little joy in her parenting. She didn't think she would feel this way as a parent.

She was constantly at odds with herself and her son, who was just over a year old before she found her way to Peaceful Parenting.

With tremendous courage, a desperate call for help, and a big, deep breath, Lina let go. She stopped trying so hard to fit the mold of what others expected of her and was determined to create a new relationship with her son. She reached out for support and moved toward change for herself and her family.

Today, she describes the absolute heart-expanding experiences she has every day with her son. She loves watching him play and simply be himself. She's proud when he says 'no' and is no longer offended by it. She recognizes that her son has a defined sense of self and is no longer operating under the people-pleasing frame that caused her so much distress in her parenting journey.

As a parenting coach today, she shares a story of a mom struggling to connect with her child and enjoy parenting. She asked this mom,

"What if you just let yourself be with him? Can you just rest into BE-ing with your kids?"

"What do you mean?" said the mom. "Like give him the iPad, and I just sit next to him with my iPhone?"

"No," said Lina, "I mean, just BE with him. Without a device, distraction, or task. Just be."

So simple and yet wholly transformative. Lina describes her journey and her new ability to help other parents shift their perspective as parents as "the biggest personal transformation ever." She LOVES parenting now. She's enjoying the moments with her son and basking in his growth as a unique, defined individual.

We have to transform the way we approach parenting. Because the old way isn't working. It's not working for parents. It's not working for kids. And the payoff could save us all.

Children are born innocent. They shine so brightly. They are truly full of light. But the way we've been parenting for generations dims that light. One notch at a time, we all get taken down. We build up defenses to protect ourselves from pain and form addictions to numb our pain.

Imagine a world where children's light was allowed to continue to shine brightly. A world where their parents act as mentors and guides to real integrity, steeped in family values. Imagine what happens when more and more people know how to feel their feelings without blaming or shaming others for them. Imagine a world where people can ask for what they need and want without shame or fear of simply having needs. Imagine a world where people are resourced with the love and support of their parents and the sense of self-worth and safety that come from knowing unconditional love.

We would transform the world for the better, and I'm here for it. How about you?

THE TEN PILLARS OF PEACEFUL PARENTING

1. Informed and aware

When practicing Peaceful Parenting, we embrace skill-building, constant learning, and a willingness to be informed of the latest research, science, and understanding of how children best develop and blossom.

We are willing to challenge conditioned and outdated modes of thinking that place expectations and responsibility on children that are developmentally inappropriate and sometimes harmful.

We embrace brain science, attachment science, nervous system science, emotional intelligence, and conscious communication.

As the parent or caregiver, we take responsibility for ourselves to understand what is happening beneath the child's behavior.

We take responsibility for assuring our family rules, boundaries, and expectations fit with the current development of our child's brain, body, and being.

Alfie Kohn, the author of *Unconditional Parenting*, urges us to "reconsider your requests." Are your expectations, requests, and demands appropriate for your child's age, development, temperament, and quality of attachment? A child's abilities can change, often within the same day (or even the same hour!). Development isn't linear, and the adult understands that.

2. Intentional and reflective

Slow Down! We view this work as an utmost priority and slow down, declutter our lives, and carve out the necessary time to make daily intentions and reflections. We soften our resistance to how much energy and effort this commitment to Peaceful Parenting requires. It's a conscious choice.

We stand in full self-responsibility as the parent in the family and reject blaming our children for our struggles and challenges in parenthood. We set daily intentions. We reflect daily on what is working, what is not working, what needs to be tweaked, how our children can be served and cared for, and what we need as parents to thrive as leaders. We see our children as individuals who may require different things from us at different times to flourish.

3. Present, committed, and devoted to imperfect authenticity

We embrace continual self-growth. We live from a space of curiosity; when we react, we respond to our reaction with curiosity and a willingness to understand. We are aware that unprocessed feelings, experiences, and stressors from childhood can feel overwhelming and cloud our ability to be present in the moment with our child or children. We are willing to take full responsibility for how we feel, think, believe, and respond or react to our child's feelings, needs, requests, and behaviors.

We actively seek and practice receiving the support we need. We release the expectation of becoming a perfect parent and instead commit ourselves to continuous growth, awareness, and accountability. We parent for the future well-being of our child, not for immediate gratification or ease. These are not mutually exclusive, though our priority is the long-term relationship.

4. All feelings are valid and welcome

We are actively engaged in our emotional intelligence. We practice learning to name our emotional reactivity, feelings, and needs. We understand that there are no "good" or "bad" feelings for ourselves or our children, and we make space for all feelings. We model emotional containment by not reacting when overcome with strong emotion to the best of our capacity. We practice mindfulness of our feelings, acceptance, and non-judgment, so we can process them and allow them to pass.

5. Attuned and empathetic

We are dedicated to attuning to our children's experiences. We are willing to practice wondering and exploring how our children may feel and what their experience may be. We are soft, warm, and willing to offer gentle, considerate responses to our child's big feelings, disoriented actions, and mistakes.

We understand that we are responsible for our feelings and can separate how we feel from how our child feels. We are willing to look beneath any behavior as our child's best attempt to meet their needs, communicate their experience, and cope with their big feelings. We are willing to practice self-empathy, increasing our awareness and acceptance of our emotional experiences: our feelings, needs, thoughts, and beliefs.

6. Loving-kindness and forgiveness

We notice where we can soften our harshness into kindness, unconditional acceptance, and a willingness to forgive (ourselves and others).

We practice generous assumptions and reject assuming our child makes choices intentionally, willingly, out of spite or manipulation, malice, or ill will.

We generously assume our children are always doing their best: Their behavior is communication, not manipulation.

We see conflict and mistakes as opportunities to connect, learn, and grow. We remember that mistakes are a natural part of growth and development.

7. Communication to connect and understand

When practicing empowered parenting, we are dedicated to unlearning communication programming rooted in judgment, criticism, blame, shame, and projection. We are willing to learn and practice nonviolent, compassionate communication within our heads and with our children. Alfie Kohn calls this *"talk less, ask more."*

We practice daily, taking ownership of our feelings and needs and communicating directly, compassionately, and with curiosity. We will hold space for our children as they find their voices and make space for them to be heard.

8. Nonviolence and safety

We commit to nonviolence in thought, word, and deed. We aim to keep our household a space of warmth, comfort, and peace. This includes communication, clear limits, empathetic support, and creative problem-solving when we need help in our parenting. We practice nonviolence with ourselves through self-empathy, compassion, and forgiveness when we cross a boundary of safety and respect with our child. We are dedicated to reaching out for support when we realize we depend on forceful and disrespectful parenting tactics. Support is the goal, not shame.

9. Boundaries from family values

We are dedicated to setting limits, rules, and boundaries from the clarity of our core values. We are confident in knowing when to stand firm with our boundaries and when it is safe and appropriate to soften into flexibility.

We take responsibility as adults to support our children's needs, whatever they may be, at any age, to meet those expectations and boundaries. We are an active and engaged participant in our boundaries being honored. When a boundary creates conflict, we are willing to get curious about how vital that boundary truly is to us and consider our children's worldview.

10. Joy, play, and fun!

We are dedicated to unearthing and celebrating the essence of parenting: Raising children can be fun! We learn to soften conflict through connective play. We embrace play as our children's process for understanding, healing, and transforming stressed behavior into self-connected and cooperative behavior. We prioritize joy and laughter when stress and fatigue overwhelm the family culture.

We think of parenting as an opportunity to partner with our children and empower them. We understand we have the incredible honor of guiding, teaching, and supporting them in becoming their unique, authentic, and beautiful selves.

GIDEON, AGE 17

How are you aware that the way you've been parented is different than your peers?

I believe how I have been parented allows for more transparency in my relationship with my parents, creating a safer place to have a deeper connection. Whereas what I see in my peers' relationships with their parents it's very surface level with not a whole lot of connection in the sense of trust and communication.

What is the biggest difference this has made in your relationship with your parents or your life?

There are many, but the most prominent would have to be my emotional connection to my parents. It has gotten to a point where I can say what's on my mind and share my thoughts and feelings without feeling those things will be used against me. It truly feels as if my parents are some of my best friends.

What's been good about it?

Getting to know my parents better and the other way around has been beneficial in every way possible for relationships as important as these.

What's been challenging?

Taking the time and space to find the trust to really get down to the root of the cause without things turning into a perpetual cycle of arguments.

What would you want parents who are thinking about not using punishments or consequences with their kids to know?

Be patient; think about how you felt as a child/teenager; what were the things you were looking for to have a smoother relationship with your parents. Come to a middle ground.

What differences do you notice between the relationship you have with your parent(s) and the relationship of your friends who were parented more traditionally with their parents?

I notice almost 99% of the time that parents know NOTHING about their child or their mental state. It's like two different people, the one their parents think they know and then the person they are when they feel they can be authentic.

CHAPTER SIX

The Foundations of Peaceful Parenting

If you're going to play a new game, you need to understand the rules. Making the shift to Peaceful Parenting is no different. We've just got to know some things before we begin. So in this chapter, we will lay out the three most essential teachings that, in our experience of coaching tens of thousands of parents, allow parents to do parenting differently.

These foundational pillars are the building blocks of everything we teach at Jai. Ashley shares that if she hadn't learned these pieces, nothing would have worked to change her behavior.

She shares, "I was just sure about how things should be! I was sure my children should follow the rules and do what I wanted them to do. For example, I work from home downstairs while my husband is upstairs. And because my kids are upstairs, it's very easy for them to come down to Mommy's office, even during my meetings. This used to drive me crazy.

My son would come down, and I'd snap, "Mommy is working! You need to go upstairs right now!' Of course, he would persist, often leading to lots of tears on his part and frustration and overwhelm on mine. Working while parenting is crazy hard! Well, once I understood that it is a normal human need for a child to want a close connection with their caregivers, along with the implications on the nervous system when a child is stressed, it became easy to shift this pattern."

"Today," she continues, "my child will come down to the office, I'll take a few minutes to give him the connection he desires, and off he'll go back to play upstairs. Everyone is so much happier. There's no drama about it."

Much of the success that we hear about from parents is described in these micro-moments. These everyday experiences show us that things are no longer the way things were. It's when your kids don't get in a fight, or something happens, where you would have lost it in the past, but you don't. It's the moments of pure love when you can experience a profound sense of joy by simply watching your child be themself.

And the way you get to enjoy these micro-moments is to learn how you operate, how your child works, and to decide for yourself how you want to take this information and incorporate it into your everyday interactions with your child.

So let's dive into Foundation One.

FOUNDATION ONE: SELF-REGULATION

Most of our worst parenting moments don't happen on purpose. We don't usually think about yelling at our child and then decide to do it. Something happens, and then we yell. This is nervous system dysregulation. By and large, we are a reactive bunch, we humans. We either think we can't control our reactivity, or we've tried to stuff, quiet, or hold in our reactivity in the past (which actually causes more reactivity).

So basically, we are asking our kids to behave in ways that keep us from reacting because we don't like how it feels to yell or storm off or give our kids the silent treatment (and let's be honest, they don't like it either). But our reactivity isn't their responsibility—it's ours. And it's not true that we can't change our reactive natures. This is a very learnable skill!

In *Man's Search for Meaning*, Viktor Frankl writes, "Between stimulus and response, there is space. In that space is our power to choose our response. In our response lies our growth and our freedom."

Everything we need to know about nervous system regulation lives in this life-as-we-know-it-changing quote.

Before we learn how to change it, it's important to understand the nervous system and how it functions.

The autonomic nervous system's main job is to signal to our body and brain whether we are surrounded by safety or threat. The nervous system consists of the brain, spinal cord, sensory organs, and all the nerves that connect these organs with the rest of the body. Together, these organs are responsible for the control of the body and communication among its parts.

When our physiology and nervous system have been enduring chronic, prolonged stress (which—let's face it—pretty much applies to all humans), our signal receptors begin to translate safe cues as dangerous. Our nervous system is also highly dependent on our physical state, so our ability to stay regulated suffers when we haven't slept, eaten, or are under stress that isn't even related to the thing that's stressing us out.

So:

1. Because of chronic stress, we are conditioned to live in a constant underlying state of dysregulation.
2. Our lives don't help because we are too busy to eat, too anxious to sleep, and too worried about work.

This means our kids are often the proverbial straw that breaks the camel's back. Looking at it through this lens, we can recognize that:

- Our child crying in the car seat is not dangerous, but we would do anything to escape as if the car was on fire.
- Our teen telling us that they get to "make their own decisions—it's MY LIFE!" is not dangerous, but our body feels like it's facing a saber-toothed tiger and needs to prime for an attack.
- Our children bickering with each other is not dangerous, but we feel like we're going to explode (and often do!).

This is all nervous system DYS-regulation. It can all feel like too much for our frayed nervous system, but is it?

Suppose we are not aware of or connected to our autonomic nervous system—especially the cues of our internal physiology. In that case, we cannot access consciousness and conscious choice when triggered. We are at the mercy of our reactivity. And the tragic consequence of this is that our children suffer the consequences.

Good news: It doesn't need to be this way. You can absolutely learn to regulate your nervous system, and it will feel oh so good!

Step One: Embrace dysregulation

Yep. I said it. Embracing dysregulation might seem like a paradox given the perils of dysregulation and how it often has us behave in ways that don't feel good to us or our kids. But the truth? We are all going to experience dysregulation. Once we accept this for ourselves and embrace that sometimes we will feel less than Zen, the idea of returning to a regulated state gets so much easier.

If you met our coach, Allyn, you'd never imagine she could ever "lose it." Like, ever. From my perspective, Allyn is the consummate professional. She's articulate, brilliant, and calm. So when Allyn told me that she's a yeller, I was a tad surprised!

She recently shared a recent story of leaving a voice message for a fellow Jai coach while driving. A car unexpectedly drove through a stop sign, and Allyn lost it! Swearing up a storm, Allyn continued the message to her colleague "Ok, now that I'm completely dysregulated, I'm going to go take a minute . . . call you back."

Her friend called back (and was under the same impression about Allyn as I was!). "Oh my goodness, I am so relieved," she shared, "that you lose it sometimes, too!" They had a good laugh that two experts in the field of teaching nervous system regulation both still lose their minds from time to time.

We all do. The goal here is not to become unemotional or to never be triggered. For 99% of us, that's simply an unrealistic goal.

When we think we aren't supposed to get triggered, we beat ourselves up for being triggered, which only makes us more triggered. So let's embrace our dysregulation as the first step in this process. Things are going to piss you off. Heck, your kids are going to piss you off. It's ok. You have a nervous system that will set you off from time to time.

We want to learn to accept this inevitability while learning new ways to experience any disruption in our nervous system so that we don't cause harm (emotional or physical) to ourselves or others.

Here's a piece of news: You have a body, and in that body, you experience sensations.

In Western culture, we tend to live in our heads. Most people I have coached over the last twelve years experience life from the neck up. When we experience emotions, we go right to our heads. We spin up stories, defenses, and reactions and then continue to think thoughts that validate, enforce, and defend the thought patterns running through our minds and spilling out of our mouths (often through yelling, lecturing, or what I've fondly come to recognize as parent-splaining). This (I'm sorry to share this hard-to-swallow truth with you... And also not sorry, because it is indeed the truth) puts us in a victim mindset.

Deep breath. It is hard to acknowledge that we've been playing the role of the victim in our lives. It is not an easy label to accept for ourselves. So let me show you why this is: Anytime we place our hopes for happiness, fulfillment, calm, or peace of mind outside of ourselves, we are playing the role of the victim. This is because we allow the things that happen *to* us to dictate our life experiences.

Of course, bad things happen in life. When they do, it's ok to feel sorry for ourselves. We are sometimes victims of a crime, an accident, an illness, etc., and this is a separate conversation.

But when our child makes us feel something less than how we want to feel, we are not their victim. We are their parent.

Ok, so back to this body stuff because it leads us to the next step. Once we acknowledge that we will be dysregulated at various times in our lives, we want to learn to process that dysregulation for ourselves. As we take responsibility for our inner experience, we transform from the victim position into becoming the victor of our regulation.

Step Two: Feeling your feelings in your own body

Let's define dysregulation: It is the normal experience of your nervous system escalating. Depending on the specific feeling of dysregulation, you may trigger your nervous system's fight, flight, or freeze response, or you may feel despondent, heavy, and sluggish.

These feelings result from the hormones that flood your body when you get triggered. You may be flooded with cortisol and adrenaline, or you may have a disruption of the hormones that are responsible for feeling calm and happy: serotonin, dopamine, or norepinephrine. As you have an experience, let's say your children are bickering in the back seat of the car while you're stuck in crazy traffic, these hormones flood your body through your limbic system.

They cause some sensations in your body. You might feel heat rising in your face. You might feel a tightening in your chest or an increase in your heart rate. Your jaw may clench, or your stomach might knot up.

Becoming aware of these sensations in your body is the path to freedom from reactive victimhood. As you focus your attention inward on the physical sensations of what is happening to you, you'll give your nervous system what it needs to allow this event to move through your body in a healthy way.

As you learn to break the habit of going right to your head when you feel something and shift your attention to your body, you take a powerful step toward the life-changing skill of self-regulation.

Self-regulation is the goal. It puts you in the driver's seat of your own emotional experience. Returning to the Viktor Frankl quote, this is how we create the space he speaks of—the space that lives between stimulus and response—in which we can find our freedom. Self-regulation isn't something many of us were explicitly taught when we were children—how to notice sensations and manage the ups and downs of our emotions—and thus, it is a skill sorely lacking in many adults today.

When we talk about brains and childhood development in young children and even teens, to a certain extent, you'll learn that they do not have the capacity to self-regulate yet. They rely on us to co-regulate (More on this in Chapter Nine). But for now, know that we cannot support our children to co-regulate when we are dysregulated.

James, one of our incredible dads here at Jai, shared that being able to stay regulated despite whatever chaos is happening in his world (his kids are four and six... chaos is a normal daily occurrence!) is one of the most profound gifts of this work.

He shared a micro-moment where he was unloading the dishwasher late one night. His wife, Renee, had gone to bed early after a hard day with the kids. As he turned around to put a dish away, he stepped on a Lego (those damned Legos! Getcha every time!), yowled in pain, and dropped the dish. So yeah, he became dysregulated.

He shared how in the past, he would have yelled for Renee. He would have resented that she went to bed early and left him the kitchen to clean, that he'd been at work all day providing for the family. He would have been irritated with his kids for not picking up after themselves, again!

But this didn't happen.

He tended to his dysregulation. He put some ice on his foot. He used the tools of regulation that worked best for him. He calmed down.

And then, gratitude washed in. He remembered how hard of a day it had been for Renee. He remembered that his young children wouldn't be playing with Legos in just a few years (he also has a teenage daughter from a previous marriage). He grabbed a broom. Cleaned up the mess. Finished the dishes. And went to curl up next to his sleeping wife, feeling proud that he could give her this much-needed rest.

Life. Changing. Stuff. These micro-moments.

Learning to feel your feelings in your body takes practice, but once you learn how effective this is, you'll do it more and more naturally.

There's an added benefit here—something I only discovered through exploring how feelings feel in my body. There is so much wisdom in our feelings. We can access profound inner truths and distinctions when we let ourselves feel our bodies and get curious about the sensations of our emotions.

Sometimes I'm sad. And I don't know why. I notice that I feel heavy and lack my normal get-things-done attitude. In the past, I would have either come up with a story about the sadness and most likely blamed it on someone else (oops, sorry, ex-husband!) or numbed the feeling with my addiction to busyness or a glass of wine.

Now, I pause. I get curious. I let myself feel what is happening in my body. And after a minute or two, a truth bomb will drop in. For example: "I'm sad because my daughter had a hard experience with a friend yesterday." Teenagers have a hard time with friends sometimes. This is simply a part of their experience. This awareness is enough. I start to feel better pretty quickly once I identify the source of my sadness. No stories required. And in this example, no action is required either.

If you'd like support with this, you can find a short video and visualization exercise at www.jaiinstituteforparenting.com/book-resources

Step Three: Find regulation tools that work for you

There are things you can do to support yourself in creating nervous system regulation. Different people like different tools. One of our coaches loves washing the dishes with her full presence, feeling the warm water wash over her hands, and enjoying the bubbles popping in the sink. This is not my preferred activity, but to each his own.

For me, I get a lot of relief from physically soothing myself. I'll gently rub the top of my arms or give myself a gentle hug. I like running my hands down the sides of my face as if I was tending to a child.

If time allows, walking outside or connecting to nature, even briefly, is a very regulating choice. Humming, singing songs, or dancing it out to your favorite tune can be a great way to bring yourself back to a calm, regulated state.

And let's not forget the breath. Allowing yourself a deep, cleansing, cooling breath or three is very effective.

Here's our favorite menu of self-regulating tools. Feel free to experiment with these and find the tools that work best for you!

→ Slow, rhythmic, diaphragmatic breathing.
→ Splashing cold water on your face or taking a cold shower stimulates the dive reflex, which is associated with stimulating the vagus nerve. You can also achieve the same effect by holding a Ziplock bag filled with ice cubes against your face and holding your breath. Or submerge your tongue in cold liquid.
→ Humming or making a "vooooooo" or "om" sound stimulates the vocal cords and facilitates long, slow exhalation.
→ Running your tongue across the top of your palate or using your tongue to rub your lips.
→ Prosody is the act of speaking slowly, rhythmically, and melodically as if you're soothing a young child or pet.

→ Spending time in nature.

→ Thinking positive thoughts about other people.

→ Engaging in positive social relationships.

→ Laughing out loud! A full belly laugh stimulates the vagus nerve and is contagious.

→ Engaging in prayer or meditation.

→ Mild exercise stimulates gut flow and the vagus nerve.

→ Massages can stimulate the vagus nerve, even gently massaging around the carotid sinus on the sides of your neck.

→ Gargling activates the vagus nerve by activating the muscles in the back of the throat while exhaling slowly.

→ Cultivating healthy intestinal bacteria using probiotics.

ANCHOR: A guide through self-regulation

This framework can be your guide through a stress response or painful moment.

With practice, this will help you find safety and presence in your body, so you can show up and offer relational, emotional, and physical safety for your child. Safety and calm are *always accessible* somewhere within you. We are practicing our ability to find our way back to safety and calm whenever necessary. Your child benefits from witnessing your process of finding inner safety. It's okay for them to see you struggle and work through stress and overwhelm you back into self-control and choice.

This is healthy modeling of self-regulation. Feel free to post this all around your home and practice it as often as needed. You can remember it literally or visualize yourself dropping a physical ANCHOR during high stress or conflict. We will explore this more deeply in Chapter Eight!

IN THE MOMENT OF TRIGGER, or when you feel yourself rising in your thermometer:

- Awareness of body
- Name what is happening in your body
- Connect to your sensory calming tool
- Honor the process
- Open to connection
- Recommit to your child and present moment

FOUNDATION TWO: UNDERSTAND CHILDHOOD DEVELOPMENT

It seems a little silly but important to state, that one of our goals in Peaceful Parenting is to give our children's brains the best environment possible to develop, grow, and mature into adulthood.

While our minds aren't the best place to process emotions, as described above, they are literally the key to our children's future experiences. Brains that are nurtured become their powerful allies in a child's path to creating a life of fulfillment, impact, and purpose. So, in the same way, we try to give our children healthy food to nourish their bodies, it's important to understand what we need to give them to nourish their minds as they move through different developmental stages.

Far too often, we encounter parents who expect that children have the same brains as adults and should therefore act accordingly. I recently traveled from Cape Cod back to Boston on a ferry ride. The seats faced one another with tables in the middle, and the boat was quite crowded. I was delighted to see two remaining seats across the table from a mother and young toddler. I do love babies! This little guy wanted to tool around the boat as we left the dock. He wanted to crawl on the floor and grab almost everything he laid his eyes on! Mama was doing everything she could to get him to sit still and stop touching things, and he wasn't having it.

"Jacob," she exclaimed, "you need to behave. See all of the people on this boat? They all need you to behave. Be a good boy!" Her frustration was clearly building.

My heart ached for them both. Jacob was maybe 18-24 months old. These words? They might have been the "right words" that "good parents" say. I could feel how much this young woman wanted us all to know that she was a good mother. What I knew was that her words, albeit well-intentioned, were futile. This little guy's brain wasn't ready for words.

When we have a basic understanding of how brains develop and work as our children grow, we are better equipped to meet them appropriately in their development.

The frustration we feel with a pre-verbal toddler for not listening is tempered when we understand that a pre-verbal toddler shouldn't be expected to listen.

A basic understanding of how the brain grows and develops creates so much more peace in our homes because we can understand how to interact with our children age-appropriately. There is also some brain science that is useful for us to understand all people!

So let's talk about brains.

In the most simplistic terms, the brain stem controls our essential life functions, like breathing, heart rate, and digestion. The middle part of the brain is called the cerebellum. Its function coordinates voluntary muscle movements and maintains posture, balance, and equilibrium. And then finally, we have the cerebrum, where higher brain functions like speech, reasoning, and creativity live.

The brain develops in children from the inside out and isn't fully developed until they are in their mid-twenties!

Our brains are amazing. They take a lot of energy, though, so they are hard-wired for efficiency. The inner brain is responsible for keeping us alive, so it is always online. If our safety is threatened or we are awash in fight-or-flight chemicals, our brains will pull power from the outer regions of our brains and focus all of the available energy on survival.

Whether we are triggered, our spouse or partner is triggered, or our teenager is triggered, our brains act with a child's capacity. This is a huge thing to understand because we can stop trying to reason with an emotionally activated person, knowing that they simply can't be reasonable. The implications of this understanding impact every single relationship in our lives, which is why the first pillar of nervous system regulation matters so much.

Before we get into the generalized phases of brain development, I want to make one additional point clearly and concisely: Fear and stress inhibit growth and delay the development of the child's emotional regulatory centers and prefrontal cortex. This means that when children are living in a perpetual state of stress, worry, and anxiety (which is often the normal outcome of traditional parenting), their brains do not develop as well as if we make it a priority to mitigate and minimize their stress, worry, and anxiety.

Stress is always going to be a part of life. When balanced with a good dose of connection, peace, and inner well-being, stress can be a powerful tool for learning and growth. Since life, school, and growing up will give our children plenty of opportunities to experience stress, perhaps we can claim, with confidence, the role of being the people in our children's lives who do not cause undue stress and worry. My deep desire is that you use this knowledge as a way to abandon the ideas that parents giving their children tough love or pushing them to achieve are effective parenting.

I fell into this trap recently with my child. My kids attended a small Montessori school on a farm until eighth grade. They received the gift of spending time outdoors and following their passions and creative ideas. They knew their teachers by their first names and loved learning. There are limited opportunities for alternative high schools where we live, so Myles went to our public high school in the ninth grade. Re-entering the "real world" kicked in my competitive, achievement-oriented belief system. My mom had an "Ivy League or bust" mentality when I was in high school, and I had not done the work on this belief, as it hadn't yet reared its ugly head.

In any case, the transition proved incredibly difficult for Myles. He was socially isolated and hadn't had to sit at a desk or be loaded up with homework. He started having panic attacks and insomnia. And I, it breaks my heart to say, pushed harder. I insisted that he get involved in the school and harped on him to join a sport or club. He loves jujitsu, and I made him join the wrestling team.

He hated it. Like, really, really hated it. He was being bullied and tormented. The panic attacks escalated to a scary place. Luckily, I've got about a thousand parenting coaches to call on, and after a few calls with one of our coaches, I could see what was creating this situation: Me.

The anxiety that Myles was experiencing was crippling. His academics began to deteriorate, and if I'm being frank, there were a few weeks where I checked on him regularly throughout the night because I was scared he would harm himself.

His brain was under assault, and I have to own that my interactions with him were the perpetrator. I surrendered and gave him back the wheel of his experience. He still doesn't love high school. But he is at peace.

Rather than being the safe harbor for Myles, I became the cause of harm. We learned, together, that this would not be an effective way forward for Myles, our relationship, or his future path in life. When I stopped applying pressure, his anxiety and worry calmed down. When

I stopped pushing and being so controlling, his brain calmed down, the anxiety decreased, and the panic attacks stopped.

Today, he spends a lot of time in the woodshop, hand-making beautiful furniture and gifts. His creativity is back, and it is beautiful. It's useful to be mindful of how we are tending (or not) to our children's brains.

✳

(The following information is a general guideline, not a way to measure the achievement of developmental milestones. This also does not consider neurodiversity or other medical or psychological diagnoses that may impact development. Every child is unique and will have their own experience of maturing into adulthood.)

By becoming aware of our child's brain development, we can have more peace, congruence, and success in our parenting. We will no longer expect our child to be able to exist and deliver impossible behaviors for their development, which can create so much frustration with our child through no fault of their own.

Low Brain: Beginning at birth and coming to maturation around ages 2 or 3

The body is the main focus of development. Physical coordination is developing. The child constantly seeks safety and takes in their environment like a sponge. They are learning patterns and language. When stressed, children in this age range cannot follow verbal cues, have very little impulse control, and are 100% dependent on co-regulation to calm their bodies and contain their emotional experiences without reacting.

Mona Delahooke, in her book *Beyond Behaviors,* notes that "56 percent of parents believe that children have the impulse control to resist the desire to do something forbidden before age three. The truth: Toddlers don't start developing these abilities until age three and a half or four at the *earliest*." This is why asking a child under four to follow a spoken rule is like asking a dog to read. At this age, redirection and play are far more effective.

Middle Brain: Beginning around age 3 and coming to maturation between ages 7-12

Feelings and emotions are the main focus of development. Children are learning how to contain emotions and identify feelings. The child is still completely dependent on co-regulation when stressed. The middle brain holds our emotional regulatory centers and our impulse control. These are just beginning to develop and will require consistent warmth, empathy, modeling, and compassion to develop fully. The middle brain operates at the alpha and theta brain wavelengths, which are similar to a hypnotic state. Our belief systems are formed during this time. Supportive and life-enhancing beliefs are formed when the system feels safe and calm. Limiting beliefs are formed when the system does not feel safe and the brain is stuck in the amygdala (stress, fear, aggression, shame) and hippocampus (memory).

Frontal Lobe/Prefrontal Cortex: Beginning around age 7-12 and coming to maturation about the age of 25

Beginning at age 7, if the brain has integrated fully into a warm and safe environment, the prefrontal cortex, or the front of the brain, **begins** to develop. *The frontal cortex does not truly take flight until adolescence,* when the teenage brain is restructuring itself and experiencing a rapid pruning of old synapses and neurons and a rebirth of neural pathways. (*Brainstorm* by Daniel Siegel is an excellent resource for the teenage brain.)

→ *What occurs in the prefrontal cortex:*
→ Foresight and consideration of the future
→ Understanding of cause and effect

- → Problem-solving strategies
- → Organizing thoughts
- → Inhibiting aggressive or violent behavior
- → Impulse control and delayed gratification
- → Emotional self-regulation
- → Psychological flexibility
- → Focusing attention
- → Understanding reasoning
- → Ability to follow directions with clarity (The ability to switch from what THEY want to what YOU want or what is needed at that moment for the well-being of all.)
- → Ability to follow a multiple-sequenced direction (Example: put shoes on, put a coat on, grab lunch box; this is not activated until a child is 11 years old, and if the child has developed within warmth and security.)
- → Ability to regularly understand hypothetical reasoning and abstract concepts
- → Empathizing and truly understanding how their actions impact another

FOUNDATION THREE: CULTIVATING EMOTIONAL INTELLIGENCE

Emotional intelligence is at the core of the work that we do here at the Jai Institute for Parenting. Based on a tremendous amount of research over the last thirty years, we know that EQ (emotional intelligence) is a higher indicator of success than IQ (intellectual intelligence). And so, we embrace this knowledge in our work and see powerful shifts when parents learn to speak what we call "the language of feelings and needs."

Emotional intelligence is the capacity to feel our feelings fully, articulate and express them clearly, and handle them in a way that does not cause harm to ourselves or others.

Our culture emphasizes intellectual intelligence, which served us well through the industrial age. But we have evolved. Success in life today is far more dependent on a person's ability to communicate, cooperate and create.

Intelligence matters. It reflects our abilities, strength, and aptitude. We all have intellectual gifts to bear in our ability to solve problems.

However, we operate within the silo of our individual intelligence without emotional intelligence. It is impossible to enjoy fulfilling relationships because we hurt others with our emotional reactivity. We make our anger or frustration their problem. This is destructive to collaboration and partnership. It is also destructive to children.

By learning to make our emotions our responsibility, we do the life-changing work of being able to stay in a relationship with others (whether they are our spouse, child, co-worker, or employee) and stay rooted in solution-oriented thinking and relating.

Emotional intelligence is also a tremendous tool for reducing stress, anxiety, and worry. It is also essential for effective leadership and being someone people want to follow.

When we have low emotional intelligence, we typically boil our experience down to feeling "good" or "bad." And we look outside of ourselves to identify what is making us feel this way, giving it all of the credit—or the blame. We are reactive to circumstances versus being attuned to what is really happening.

Imagine a mom who has just had a stressful day at work. Her boss yelled at her. A client was upset. And she hasn't slept well in days.

She comes home, feels bad, and is immediately confronted with her brooding teenage daughter. Unbeknownst to Mom, her daughter also had an awful day. A close friend found out she has a crush on the friend's ex-boyfriend and is trying to get the rest of their friend group to avoid her.

Mom feels bad. The kid feels bad.

We all know the rest of the story: Blow up. It's a recipe for disaster without emotional intelligence.

"You're so ungrateful! I work so hard for you, and all you do is give me attitude!"

The daughter tells herself that her mother is awful, storms away, and slams her bedroom door. Maybe she even yells, "I hate you!!"

But if Mom has the skills of emotional awareness and co-regulation (I'll share more about this in a moment), she meets the moment in a profoundly different way.

She acknowledges her feelings to herself.

"I am tired. Stressed. At the end of my rope."

She notices her daughter's emotional state . . . Takes a deep breath . . . And embraces curiosity and empathy:

"Hey, looks like you had a day! What's happening for you?"

Then this entire scenario unfolds differently. There is a connection between mother and daughter. There is space for communication. And maybe they decide to order a pizza and watch a movie together to decompress.

The relationship is fed instead of fired up.

My favorite story about the capacity of emotional intelligence goes back to when my kids, who are fifteen and seventeen now, were much younger. I started the Jai Institute for Parenting when they were just toddlers, so we've been working on my relationship with my emotions for a long time.

Because of this, yelling is an infrequent occurrence in how we relate to each other, so it is pretty upsetting when it does happen. Everyone cries, including me!

One day we were driving home, and the traffic was awful. The kids were probably six and eight, and they were starving. They got into an argument, and it started to escalate. I don't remember what I yelled, but I lost it, leading to tears all around.

One of the tools that we will discuss in an upcoming chapter is REPAIR. Everyone gets to make mistakes. We want to learn how to come back into connection when there is a breach. So I used these tools first to self-regulate, then to connect and communicate.

"I am sorry I yelled. I was feeling stressed, and I'm hungry too! Feeling hangry feels awful, doesn't it?" I asked my kids.

My son said, "Yes, Mama, it does feel awful. But it actually feels worse when you yell at us."

I agreed with him. "It does. It feels worse to me, too. I can imagine that it must make you feel really scared and upset! What do you think we could do differently in the future?"

And this is where it gets magical, especially when working with children, because they are incredibly adept at solution-oriented thinking when we allow them the space for collaboration and creativity.

"Well," he considered, "how about the next time you feel yelling coming up in your body, you tell us that you feel yelling coming up in your body?"

"Um. Yes. O. k. I can definitely do that!"

This is now a well-loved joke in our family. "I feel yelling coming up in my body" has served us so well, in so many ways, some of them quite funny—like the time my daughter had to have a thorn she got in a corn maze plucked out of her eye at the urgent care clinic! The medical staff got some strange looks, but it relaxed her and made us all laugh!

The breach led to connection instead of remaining an unhealthy emotional pattern that was causing harm to our family.

THREE BENEFITS OF BEING AN EMOTIONALLY INTELLIGENT PARENT

1) You are more open to new ideas and collaboration from your kids.

Low emotional intelligence makes us far more likely to believe what we think is right. We then emphatically defend what we think and are only open to evidence that supports our firmly held beliefs and ideas because of confirmation bias. We ignore opposing views and even real, factual evidence. We argue our position to the point of disempowering the very people (our kids!) we want to empower. We operate from emotional reactivity instead of responsiveness.

When we have the tools and skills of emotional intelligence, we understand that transitory emotions often drive our initial reactions. We give our thoughts and feelings time to process. We consider other perspectives and can analyze reality without being clouded by our emotional inconsistency. We don't need to be right. We consider the consequences and outcomes of ideas and form a better strategy because the ideas for solutions are a collaboration.

2) You are effective at setting and maintaining boundaries without creating resentment or resorting to power-over strategies that disempower others.

Emotional intelligence allows us to balance compassion, empathy, and kindness with clear and communicated boundaries.

We can handle our inner emotional landscape and de-personalize the situation so that we can meet our people where they are in their emotional landscape. We can give feedback, even hard feedback, without causing emotional harm. We become masterful at handling conflict.

3) Your kids will trust you.

There is no more valuable asset as a parent than the trust of your kids. Demonstrating emotional intelligence not only models a new way of being in the world but also gives our children a genuine sense of safety and well-being in your leadership.

Without EQ, we hurt others (We don't mean to; it's simply what happens.) because we are victims of our emotional reactivity. Unhealthy relationship patterns take hold. Resentment builds. We make up stories about the other person's motives, behaviors, and personality characteristics.

We simply need to open our ears in a grocery store or restaurant to witness the interplay of low EQ skills at play compassionately. We witness well-meaning parents blaming their kids for their emotions.

"If you didn't ____, I wouldn't be so pissed!"

"I paid for this vacation, so why aren't you having fun?!? You're so ungrateful!"

"You're making me so mad!"

Or the one that hurts my heart the most—a family sitting at a dinner table, separating and numbing themselves with their phones (or wine!).

The real prize of emotional intelligence is the ability to be self-aware, to notice and name our feelings, and to have empathy and compassion for the genuine emotions and feelings of others. This is intimacy.

Rather than allowing negative emotions to fester and create resentment, we can express them in healthy ways and connect with our loved ones. We create a path forward with solution-oriented communication and agree on new ways of relating that strengthen and deepen our relationships.

Unexpressed emotions fester. I always tell my kids that holding on to their feelings is far more painful than allowing them air. When we develop emotional intelligence and the ability to speak the language of feelings and needs, we give our emotions the air they need to move.

I'm sure you can think of a time (or twenty) when a situation or circumstance felt far worse in your head than when you found out the truth about it.

"Name it to tame it."

When we learn to feel our emotions, discern their root cause, remove blame and shame, and communicate effectively to the people directly involved in a situation calmly and clearly, we shift the neurochemistry of our body and brain.

Cortisol and adrenaline are replaced with the love chemicals of oxytocin, dopamine, and serotonin. These are life-extending, inflammation-reducing, and healing for the body. We develop more resilience, self-confidence, and stability, leading to a healthier mind.

THREE TOOLS TO DEVELOP A GREATER DEGREE OF EMOTIONAL INTELLIGENCE

1) Get curious about your feelings.

Self-awareness is the doorway to emotional intelligence. Without emotional intelligence, we tend to view our feelings as good or bad.

So we chase good feelings (often in self-destructive ways). And we blame other people for our bad feelings because it releases them (often in self-destructive ways).

By getting curious about our feelings, we can gain so much more access to the subtleties of our experiences. There are so many flavors of emotions. The feelings wheel we use to teach emotional intelligence has 128 feelings!

So, for example, we've all experienced being sad. As we get curious about our sadness, however, we can perhaps identify that we are feeling lonely versus feeling ashamed. Now that we are clear that we are feeling lonely, we can even go deeper and identify that we are feeling isolated versus feeling abandoned.

And then we can claim that for ourselves: "I feel isolated."

Feeling sad hurts. But there's not much information available to us to shift to solution-oriented thinking. "I feel isolated" gives us quite a bit of information. We can then discern whether this is true, clarify why we feel that way, and take measures to alleviate the situation.

The feeling becomes our greatest tool for a better experience, rather than being something we want to blame someone else for, avoid, or numb.

2) Develop Emotional Capacity

Feelings can't hurt you. They hurt, but you are simply experiencing a feeling you can handle in your body.

We are taught from a young age that we should avoid negative emotions. We learned that anger is bad. Adults told us to get over it when we were sad. We were shamed for our fears.

Since no one taught us how to feel our feelings, we avoid them. We tell ourselves stories about them. We make them other people's responsibility.

I have a powerful secret to share with you. The more adept and practiced you become at feeling hard emotions, the more joy, love, and wonder you will experience from good emotions. We can only truly feel the good things in equal measure to our ability to feel the hard things.

It sounds trite to say, but you can handle far more than you give yourself credit for, I promise.

So here's the invitation: The next time you are feeling something . . . feel it! Sit with it. Don't think. Don't tell stories. Don't analyze it with your mind. Just feel what you're feeling IN your body.

What is the quality you are experiencing? Do you notice pressure, heat, or heaviness? Is the feeling electric or dull?

Where do you feel this? Is it in your heart, your stomach, your head?

If the feeling had a color, what would it be? If it had a shape?

Can you get more specific in naming this feeling? Here's a picture of the Feelings Wheel.

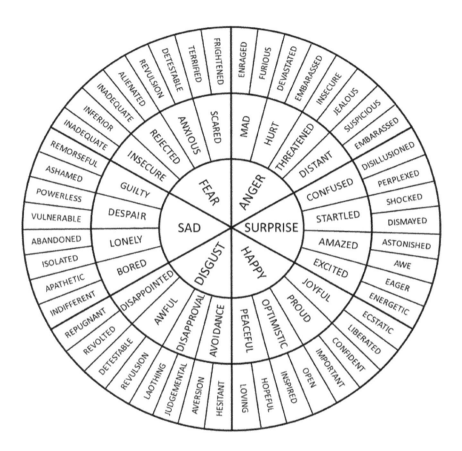

And finally, notice what happens as you meet this feeling with your awareness. Ask yourself what the feeling was telling you.

If you're like most people, you'll discover three things:

- The feeling dissipates as you feel it.
- You'll gain clarity and insights into the issue causing the feeling.
- No humans were harmed through this process!

3) Replace defensiveness with curiosity and empathy.

It is normal and oh-so-human to feel defensive. And as a parent, we can fall into the trap of needing to be right to maintain our authority and position. But we don't need to go down the rabbit hole of our defensiveness. It is rarely useful in the long term.

Instead, what if we see defensiveness as a warning sign within ourselves? Remember, the need to be right is a sign of lower emotional intelligence. It blocks us from connection and separates us from the people we are trying to lead.

The antidote? Empathy and curiosity.

Empathy is an often-misunderstood concept. The ability to empathize with another person's experience doesn't mean that we need to share their experience. We may not get it. We may have a different perspective. In the same situation, we might respond differently.

Genuine empathy is holding space for another person's experience, feelings, emotions, and perceptions without filtering them through our worldview. It is the ability to see their experience through their worldview, without judgment, giving advice, or trying to fix anything. It is pure presence.

When my son was a toddler, he would wake up screaming at three a.m. The situation? Dire. The red Lego was on top of the blue Lego. He desperately needed this to be remedied. Because clearly, the blue Lego should have been on top. Now, through our adult lens, we can laugh (or get really frustrated) by the inanity of his upset. But for him, in his three-year-old world, it mattered. A lot.

Chris has a daughter with autism. She's loved twinkle lights since she was little. In fact, 'lights' was her only spoken word for the first few years of her life. Recently, Maddie, now in her twenties, decided to decorate the backyard with twinkle lights. Chris's first thought? The electricity bill and the idea that maybe this wasn't the best use of her daughter's time. But she ran her reaction through her empathy lens and remembered the joy Maddie has always gotten from lights. Her reaction dissipated easily and quickly.

Curiosity is the gateway to empathy and a Peaceful Parenting super-power. Curiosity asks, "I wonder what is happening with my child?" When we insert this pause into our self-talk before we start scolding our child, we often find ourselves in an entirely different state. We move from reactive to aware. This ultimately means we do much less correcting and far more connecting.

When we embrace our role as an emotionally intelligent parent, we can become more compassionate to others who might not have the same tools and skills with their emotional experience. Just as we don't get angry with a baby for not knowing how to walk, it's not helpful to others to be triggered by their big feelings. When a baby is learning to walk, we are patient as they try and fall down and try again. Perhaps we make it a game by placing their favorite toy just out of arm's reach as they pull themselves up on the coffee table.

Having emotional intelligence as a parent means that we understand the emotional reactivity that may present in others. We don't take it personally. We don't get into the mud with them. We do the work to stay regulated within ourselves, providing a safe environment for their emotional expression. And then, once everyone is calm, we can redirect toward solutions.

There is tremendous humility (and courage) involved in this learning, but it is the best hope we have to raise children with emotional intelligence. Because the old saying had it wrong: Children don't do as we say. They do as we do.

OLIVIA, AGE 15

How are you aware that the way you've been parented is different than your peers?

It's only recently that I've been aware that the way I've been parented is different than other kids. Because growing up, I've just felt very loved and respected, and I thought, I don't know... That everyone did.

But I guess that's not really the case. I can feel that I am loved and respected and I feel like that's really the most important thing for teachers, parents, and other adults in kids' lives. Because I've been respected, I give respect back. And so, as I've gotten older, I can see how kids haven't really been respected.

What is the biggest difference this has made in your relationship with your parents or your life?

I can talk to my parents more. There's more trust, and I can speak to them about anything, open up to them. We just have really good times. We make time for each other.

What's been good about it? What's been challenging?

My parents have taught me a lot of things with their knowledge that I feel like if we weren't so close and didn't have as much respect for each other, we wouldn't have gone into the conversations that we've had together.

I think many of our challenges are just the normal stuff between parents and kids, but I do think they understand what I'm going through at the age I'm in.

What would you want parents who are thinking about not using punishments or consequences with their kids to know?

I didn't grow up with punishments, so I don't know if they are bad. But I think understanding where the kids are coming from is important because if you don't, then you don't have a reason to punish them. I don't think people need punishments. Just talking it out is key.

What differences do you notice between the relationship you have with your parent(s) and the relationship of your friends who were parented more traditionally with their parents?

Even though I grew up in Waldorf, some kids went through the punishments, and I think what I see is that they are more, kind of, aggressive and maybe less sure of who they are. I don't really know if, like, that's because they were punished, but that is what I notice.

CHAPTER SEVEN

The Discipline R(E)volution

Lina admits with hesitation that before having kids of her own, she had made all sorts of declarations about what she would and would not do as a mother. Lina had spent plenty of time looking after her three nieces, so she thought she knew what to expect.

Lina discovered how wrong she had been about what it would be like as soon as she gave birth to her first son. All the self-imposed expectations she had set came crashing down. Between the brain fog and all the contradictory advice she was receiving from every direction, Lina was completely overwhelmed and felt deeply resentful that she could not return to work. That's when she reached out to Jai.

Through our parent coaching program, she was able to slow down long enough to connect more deeply to what she wanted for herself and her family. She examined and articulated her values in a way she never had before. She and her husband also got together and clarified their shared family values.

One of those values is freedom. For Lina and her husband, that means allowing their children the freedom to be who they choose to be in speech and behavior. Recently, she entered her kitchen, and her little guy was standing on the counter, reaching for a box of cookies on a shelf. She trusted that he could keep himself safe and anchored to her value of 'freedom.' She snapped a quick photo and posted it on her social media. A friend commented: "My child would never do that." Because Lina was anchored to the value, she didn't take it personally and didn't feel judged. Part of working with our values is understanding that they may look different than other people's.

According to Lina, this has been incredibly liberating. Now when her son is 'misbehaving,' she reframes his behavior as exercising his freedom to be himself. It gives her the strength to buffer any judgment she might experience in those moments from family members or friends who might not share her same values.

Discipline matters. But not in the traditional way that we might think about it. The discipline that we want to cultivate in our children is self-discipline. We want children to be intrinsically motivated to do the right thing at the right time, even when no one is watching. We want them to know how to take care of themselves and others, emotionally and physically. We want them to be contributors to our family, community, and, someday, their own family, and hopefully the world.

When children are disciplined (or shunned) because they break a rule or cause us frustration, aggravation, humiliation, or fear, we aren't instilling the life lessons that will empower them to develop intrinsic motivation as they mature. We are essentially conditioning their behavior to avoid imposed consequences.

Parents often enforce consequences because they don't know where else to turn. Enforced consequences (like taking away a favorite toy or privileges or using strategies like timeouts) work in the short-term to moderate behavior. In a way, they work. But (and this is a BIG BUT) it's crucial to understand the negative effects that enforcing consequences can have on children.

Threats and fear-based discipline can have several unintended harms:

- They can lead to power struggles and resentment.
- The child learns how to behave to avoid punishment, not because they understand the values or morals we are trying to teach.
- The use of consequences can often be inconsistent and unpredictable, leading to confusion and a lack of emotional safety for the child.
- Threats and fear-based discipline can cause the child to feel unsafe or anxious around their parents, and as children grow older, it teaches them to hide behaviors and activities that they know will get them into trouble.
- It damages the trust within the parent-child relationship.

With cutting-edge research rooted in neuroscience and child development, we now know that the "way it's always been done" has drawbacks. More effective long-term parenting methods raise happy, fulfilled children who grow into resilient adults and allow parents to feel fulfilled and gratified through their parenting journey.

Additionally, enforcing consequences affects children's self-worth and self-esteem. These punitive methods, which, in academia, are called Achievement-Oriented Parental Control (AOC), have negative effects on both emotional and psychological well-being in children:

> Controlling parental behavior was found to have negative effects on major markers of poor socio-emotional development such as depressive feelings, behavior problems, poor conscience development, and noncom-

pliance with parents (e.g., Assor et al., 2014; Barber et al., 2005; Kim et al., 2014; Kochanska et al., 2019; Olson et al., 2002; Soenens & Vansteenkiste, 2010; Soenens et al., 2005).

According to Self-Determination Theory (SDT), children feel that their need for autonomy is impeded when their parents get them to act in specific ways. These control-oriented parenting methods do not have to be severe to have negative effects on children:

> While AOC includes these punitive practices, it also includes milder forms of control. For example, commands, repeated reminders to behave as expected that are not accompanied by threats, nonviolent physical interventions (e.g., holding and directing the child's hand to ensure success in the task), and unsolicited premature help.(Olson et al., 2002; Soenens & Vansteenkiste, 2010; Soenens et al., 2005)

Of course, enforcing consequences in parenting is effective in getting a certain behavioral goal met, but only for as long as children decide to comply based on punishments and short-term rewards. We must ask why we want our child to behave a certain way. Is it about a value, or is it about control? Is it because the behavior is merely annoying or that the behavior is unsafe? Are we unintentionally creating barriers that interfere with our child's willingness to cooperate naturally?

The best way to answer these questions is through clear, articulated, and shared family values. Knowing what the "right choices/decisions/ behaviors" are is useful as determined by our family values. Every family has the opportunity to explore the values that matter to them. Things that matter to you may not matter to a different family. And that is more than o.k.

When we identify, name, and discuss our family's values, we give ourselves a foundation for our parenting. Rather than our interactions with our children being at the mercy of our emotions, stress, and anxiety, we can run our parenting choices through our values filter and show up as a more consistent, calm, and effective parent.

Values become the north star of our work as parents. They keep us grounded in the big picture and long-term goals while providing a framework for teaching our children to make good decisions. Knowing why we want them to make these decisions creates empowerment and certainty. Before we dive into identifying the values that will guide you forward in your parenting, let's discuss some caveats.

VALUES AREN'T FIXED

One of the foundational pillars of Peaceful Parenting is being 'Informed and Aware." As discussed in Chapter Five, this pillar invites flexibility into the frame. Our values may shift and evolve. They are living, breathing ideals intended to meet the moment and not to be another thing we fixate on and use as a construct of control.

Parents may reprioritize values depending on the current situation or circumstances. For example, you may hold freedom as a value in your family. You may identify this as every family member having the right to autonomy in their choices and decisions. When your child is four, however, and exerts his freedom by hitting or biting, the value of safety supersedes the value of freedom.

Allyn shares a story to which we can all relate. When her children were young, she valued sleep as a prioritized family value. When her family didn't get enough sleep or stick as closely as possible to their sleep schedule, her kids were less cooperative and more reactive, and she had less capacity to meet them in peace and connection. (So very relatable!).

Allyn's in-laws, however, did not see the importance of getting the kids to bed on time.

While Allyn loved her in-laws and getting together for a family meal once a week, she often felt like the party pooper when she took the kids home early. She was frustrated that dinner was served late, infringing on bedtime. Even though Allyn is committed to the value of 'family connection,' she prioritized sleep while her children were very young. Standing firmly in her value of sleep helped her hold the boundary around bedtime schedules and strengthened her resolve despite any pushback from family members. She knew it was vital to their growth and development (and her sanity as a mom).

As her kids got older, their sleep schedule became less of a priority. She could then be more flexible and stay later at family dinners.

※

There will be values that matter to you, that may not matter, or matter less to your spouse or co-parent. As a Peaceful Parent, it's important to allow others (even if it's your spouse!) to care about different things than you. It's rarely useful to a relationship, intimate or otherwise, to need to be "right." So give others, including your children, space to hold, develop, articulate and request the values that matter most to them once they are old enough to contribute to the conversation.

It honors others in our life to allow them to have different values than we do. We can assess, within the context, if it's a time to assert the boundary (as in Allyn's story above) or to allow our child a different experience by letting a different value drive our decisions and choices. An example: When my kids were small, my value of enoughness (I know that's not a word, but I made it up for our family because I wanted a way to define my belief that stuff is an addiction and that my kids didn't need so much of it) was in clear conflict with my mother's value of (oh-my-gosh this sounds judgy, but I promise it's not) extravagance.

My mother loves giving us things. Gifts, vacations, fancy dinners, and tickets to shows. When the kids were young, she would show up with bags of gifts. It used to trigger the heck out of me until I realized that I would rob her of joy and connection with her grandchildren if I enforced my value over hers.

I remember many conversations with the kids about the generosity they received from my mom. Rather than making my mom wrong, I used these experiences to talk with my kids about gratitude and materialism as they got older. I asked them about their thoughts. We've explored this seeming contradiction in many ways over the years, allowing for nuance and connection through our values.

Our values also work best if they consider the specific needs of the child we are parenting. Chris has a child who is neurodiverse. When she became a parent, Chris thought that education was a primary value she would prioritize as her children grew up. But she was faced with the reality that this value was causing more harm, stress, and anxiety than was healthy for her child. To best serve her daughter's needs, Chris reprioritized her values.

Values are infinitely flexible and go far beyond their labels. They are a tool for exploration and discussion. Imagine the world if more and more parents talked to their kids about why they feel certain things are important to them and gave their children a voice in exploring these goals.

CONDITIONED VERSUS AUTHENTIC VALUES

Our goal here is to understand the basis of decision-making, family rules, and expectations. Our values are our anchors. They inform us when we need to be more assertive or allowing. But we should exercise care because sometimes we create a story that we "should" care about or are "supposed to" care about a value. When we do this, the anchor loses its purpose and leaves us exerting control over a conditioned belief. This is when insecurity arises around "am I doing the right thing?". Instead of just buying into prescribed ideas, we must move toward greater truth, clarity, and self-confidence in the values we live and embody.

Sometimes, because we are human beings who didn't always (or often) get our needs met, we are parenting from an internalized lack of that need. If we lack self-confidence, we will unconsciously "need" our child to give us confidence. If we lament the opportunities we didn't get or take in our past, we will unconsciously push our child to take advantage of opportunities. A parent can be anxiously or aggressively attached to a certain value if it was chronically unmet or dishonored in their childhood.

Our values left unexplored may be disguised defense mechanisms from our own early experiences of trauma. Ashley, who suffered sexual abuse as a child, started her journey to Peaceful Parenting with some (very understandable) feelings about safety and sexuality. As she healed, she could see that it was o.k. for her children to see her undressed and that there wasn't a predator hiding around every corner. Her defensive values softened, and her authentic values (empowerment, kindness, leadership) revealed themselves.

Here's a great litmus test: If our child is doing something that we deem in conflict with our stated value, and we have a grounded and secure attachment to that value, then we can access curiosity for our child, have a willingness to look beneath the behavior and are motivated to support our child back into alignment with the value. If, however, our child is doing something that we deem in conflict with a value, and we have inner pain attached to that value, then we will react with anger, righteousness, and power-over parenting in the name of "teaching the child a lesson." In our defensiveness, we probably won't realize that the lesson we are trying to teach is rendered ineffective, as it stems from our inner disorientation, clouded emotional perception, and painful childhood experiences.

How to differentiate conditioned or deficit values from true values:

1. **Notice how the body feels hearing their value reflected back and the thoughts associated.** If the body feels open and calm, the value is rooted in truth, safety, and secure attachment. Suppose the body feels numb or tight or experiences a rush of energy or emotion. In that case, this value is most likely linked to an emotional memory or a belief that may not be serving you to navigate boundaries with clarity and grace.
2. **Work with your spouse, co-parent, or parenting coach to examine the authenticity of your belief in each value.**

Conversation prompts:

→ *"Are any thoughts coming to your mind as we discuss this value?"*
→ *"What else do you associate with this value?"*
→ *"What does [VALUE] mean to you?"*
→ *"What does [VALUE] look like to you?"*
→ *"When your child can access your expectation of [VALUE], what needs are met for them? What belief is present?"*

3. **Check generational patterns to contextualize your values**

Conversation prompts:

→ *"I wonder, how did respect show up in your childhood home? If you were "disrespectful," how were you treated?"*
→ *"Do you notice yourself having similar rules for your kids that your parents had for you? How did those rules feel for you as a kid? How were those rules communicated to you?"*

Because of our work here at the Jai Institute for Parenting, we know that three values repeatedly arise as conditioned versus authentic, so they bear some conversation here.

Respect

Many parents want respect to be a top value in their home because it is directly linked to a tender need of their own from childhood. Their parents demanded respect from them, and so they felt a need to demand respect from their children. Respect is beautiful, necessary, and supportive in a family environment! Yet, the *attachment* to the value hooks parents into power over parenting to defend the tender space in their own experience. The demand and command that parents experience respect from their children cause separation, resentment, and bitterness (think back to your experience as a child if this resonates from your childhood). There's no right or wrong here, and there is much room for nuance.

There is powerful information available to us by simply asking the questions outlined above. My conditioned belief that I should have respect as a family value has evolved into "all voices matter in this family." When I examined this belief through the lens of curiosity, I realized that my real value was to have a culture of being heard. That culture applies to my need to be heard and honors that other family members also have a right to be heard. You get to determine the authenticity of your articulated values too.

Achievement

We are all up against a cultural force that says that our child's success will measure the quality of our parenting. Whether in athletics, academics, or popularity, our kid's results are a tricky, slippery trap that most of us fall into from time to time. Again, achievement in and of itself is not the problem. Of course, we want our children to excel and to use their innate gifts, creativity, and passion in life-affirming ways. Of course, we want them to continue to develop their strengths over time.

The achievement trap comes into play when we push them to accomplish goals to meet our needs for validation or significance. We're all, in some way, unconsciously looking for the proverbial "my kid's an honors student" bumper sticker to put on display. (If you've already done the work around disentangling this one, deep bows to you.)

Achievement can be labeled in sneaky ways. We might say that we have a value of "participating in team sports," "being musical," or even "education." But when we get honest about what we're really saying, it's achievement. When we push our kids to excel in this way, they experience conditional love. They experience that they are less worthy when they don't win the game, make the team, or get the 'A.' This robs them of their agency (the right to decide how to spend their time and energy), confidence, and self-worth. The suicide rate of teenagers in San Francisco County (home of Google and Stanford) is the highest in the country. The pressure these kids face to be the best is intolerable.

There are many shifts possible in our examination of the values that will allow our children to pursue their passions and talents without putting so much pressure on them. You might decide to be "thinkers" or to "move our bodies." You might say, "In this family, we prioritize peace over accomplishments." Again, this is for you to examine, question, and explore with your family.

Appearance

This is another conditioned value that might unconsciously hide behind the safety of other values. It also can refer to many things. It can refer to our actual appearance in terms of our clothes, makeup, or hair. It can refer to the house we live in or the car we drive. It can show up in the schools we send our kids to or the food we eat.

Ultimately, when we examine these hidey-holes, we discover that they are all about what other people think of us, which is a fairly certain path to a less-than-fulfilling life.

If we want our kids to look, act, or behave in certain ways so that things look impressive to others, then, yes, this is, by definition, a conditioned value. Relaxing our grip in these areas gives us so much more peace. We don't need to ensure our daughter's hair is brushed before going to the store. Who cares? We don't need to participate in the conversation at the playground about whose child is reading Voltaire in the second grade. We can see the projection for what it is with compassion. We can witness the need for others to use their child as a shield for their insecurities without getting into the muck with them.

The process of naming, questioning, examining, and clarifying our personal values is powerful when looking at our motivations around the decisions we make and how we spend our most precious assets: our time and energy.

WHAT ARE YOUR TOP THREE PERSONAL VALUES?

It's time to define the things that are important to you. Below is a list of widely held values. This is far from a comprehensive list but can be used to initiate the values you want to bring to your family. You may hold some values that are not on this list. Feel free to add more if you care deeply about something that is not on the list.

This exercise gives you a framework for identifying your personal values. Review the values on the attached list. Circle or mark ten values you feel are most important in your life today. You don't have to think about this too much. It is usually fairly accurate to quickly identify the values that resonate with you, move you, and jump out at you.

After you've got a personal list of top values, you'll want to simplify! Pare it down and highlight your top three.

LIST OF VALUES

Accomplishment/
Success
Authenticity
Equality
Meaning
Accountability
Fairness
Money
Accuracy
Faith/Faithfulness
Openness
Adventure
Family/Family Feeling
Oneness
Loyalty
Flair
Others' points of view
Beauty
Freedom/Liberty
Peace/Nonviolence
Calm/Quietude
Friendship
Personal Growth
Challenge
Fun
Pleasure
Change
Generosity
Perseverance

Charity
Gentleness
Power
Cleanliness/
Orderliness
Global view
Quality of work
Collaboration
Gratitude
Reliability
Commitment
Goodness
Resourcefulness
Communication
Hard work
Respect
Community
Happiness
Security
Competence
Harmony
Self-reliance
Competition
Health
Service (to others,
society)
Concern for others
Honor
Simplicity

Connection
Improvement
Skill
Cooperation
Independence
Spirit/Spirituality
in Life
Creativity
Individuality
Strength
Determination
Stability
Delight of being
Joy
Integrity
Success
Democracy
Intelligence
Teamwork
Discipline
Intensity
Tolerance
Discovery
Justice
Tradition
Diversity
Kindness
Trust

I've found it useful to create affirming statements for each value that I hold as a parent.

"We do not hurt with words, bodies, or things in our family."

"We are a family of thinkers."

"We value generosity because we know we receive more than we give."

"We are good with good enough."

Want more of our favorite values-based sayings?

Yes, your children will sometimes roll their eyes at you as they grow older. Still, these values seep into their understanding of themselves and their relationship with the world because they inform their identity. Identity drives our decisions and behaviors. We can't outmaneuver it or willpower our way through it. How we see ourselves is how we will carry ourselves through the world, whether we like it or not.

If you are partnered, it is great to have your co-parent do this exercise, too! Together, you can discover the values you share and the values you hold as individuals. Remember, there's no right or wrong here, only a deeper understanding of how we tick.

If you're really geeky about this work and it's age-appropriate, you can have a weekly family meeting where you pull out one of your family values for discussion, stories, and questions. I believe that either we intentionally teach our kids this stuff, or the world will teach it to them for us. I don't know about you, but I tend to prefer the values we hold in this family over those communicated through the media and culture.

Understanding our family values, talking about them with our kids, and most importantly, living into those values ourselves shapes, guides, and leads our children to have a strong personal identity that will serve them well throughout their lives.

We can soften our instinct to protect our children from the world when we know a defined set of values guides them. Allyn shared a story about her mom being shocked by a Disney movie that she feared would expose her grandkids to teenage rebellion. "Mom," shared Allyn, "I trust that my kids can watch this, know that things are happening in this story outside our values system, and come to me with any questions they may have."

Values-based parenting addresses so much of what is missing in traditional parenting. We effectively shift from "because I said so" to "here's why this matters."

A note: No one on the planet will call you out on an integrity breach (aka hypocrisy) faster than your kid, especially in a house where children can speak their minds and be heard. In traditional parenting, this might be interpreted as a lack of respect. But I'd rather see it as a victory. Peaceful Parenting is about parents transforming. I don't want to be a hypocrite, and I'm guessing you don't either. We are all human beings, and sometimes we're going to trip over ourselves. More on this later, but it's o.k. for our kids to let us know when they see us making decisions that seem to fly in the face of our stated family values. These moments are fertile ground for conversation, exploration, and clarification. We get to learn and grow, too!

Remember that semester Myles spent away at boarding school recently? Well, a boy in his dorm came determined to find himself a girlfriend. He was overly solicitous with some of the girls on campus and made several of them deeply uncomfortable on several occasions. Myles has been raised with the value of respecting women. On his own, he went to the headmaster to advocate for these sixteen-year-old girls. With the headmaster, he devised a plan to have a dorm meeting where they came up with a framework to "call each other out" without blame, shame, or attack when they noticed someone was causing discomfort in others. They created change. Of course, I'm proud of my kid. But more importantly, he is a living, breathing, difference-making person carrying the legacy of the values he's been gifted.

Nothing is more fulfilling than witnessing your children embody the values that you, their parent, taught them. When you see them making choices and decisions of their own free will, no lecturing, pleading, or threatening required, the eye rolls will be worth it. Values are powerful ideas that live on and continue to evolve in the children we raise.

ZEIDA, AGE 7

What do you like the most about the way your parents treat you?

I like that you're kind, that we talk about things, snuggles, and that we do things together. Mama and Papa are fun!

Have you ever been punished for doing something wrong? How would it feel to be punished?

No. It sounds scary, and I wouldn't like it.

How do you know what the rules are? Do you follow them? What happens when you don't?

By making mistakes and talking about it after, we talk about them. I do the best I can to follow the rules. Mama or Papa helps me or reminds me.

CHAPTER EIGHT

The End of Punishments and Consequences

Rebekah is the sweetest, smartest, and kindest of teenagers. And she is hurting. The youngest daughter of parents who went through a challenging and traumatic divorce, she's often the pawn used by her parents to control, hurt, and manipulate each other. Her parents can't see how they are impacting their child's self-worth. They love her, but they don't listen to her. They don't see her.

Rebekah is a friend of my daughter's. On a recent road trip, she read me a letter she'd written to her dad. It was clear to me that this child longs to be seen and understood by her parents. She strives for achievement to try to gain their attention, their affection, and their ears.

She is often at the mercy of her parents' lack of ability to communicate with each other, and her father clearly sees her through the clouded lens of his feelings about his ex-wife. This fifteen-year-old girl is communicating, but her parents aren't listening. They are telling—telling her who she is, who she should be, how she should act, and what she should think.

I'll be honest. I worry about her. Deeply. Because the first step to helping struggling kids is admitting that how we communicate with them is a problem. It's much easier to think that the child is the problem, is the one who doesn't listen, or label them as spoiled, ungrateful, or a lost cause.

Kids believe their parents and adopt an identity that says they are less than, unlovable, and unworthy of being heard.

~

Our children are going to misbehave. They are going to break the rules. They are going to test limits and boundaries. Not because they aren't good people, but because they are human. When we accept this fundamental truth, we can soften into Peaceful Parenting, which places us in the position of being our child's mentor and guide.

Many years ago, we were returning home from a visit to New York City, where we stayed in a friend's apartment who was out of town. We stopped for lunch along the way, and when I returned to the table with the food, I noticed that my son had a small brass owl figurine in his hand.

"I see that you have an owl. I haven't seen that owl before," I said. "Where did you get it?"

"Oh," he said, "I found this in the basement before we left on our trip."

"Hmmm," I said. "I notice I'm feeling sadness in my body because I don't think that is the truth. I have never seen that owl before."

He insisted that I was wrong and that the owl was ours. "I'll remind you, Myles, that in our family, it's okay to make mistakes and that when we do, we also clean them up." I left it there for the moment. Later that night, I circled back to the owl after a story.

"Myles, I want to clear something up with you. I am feeling sad and worried because I am telling myself a story that you took the owl from our friend's apartment. Is that story true?"

He started to cry. I comforted him and asked, "How would you like to make this right?"

He shared, "I think I would like to send it back with a letter to say that I'm sorry for taking the owl."

"That is a great idea. We can do that together in the morning."

We sent the package off in the morning, and a week later, Myles received a letter in the mail. It was from our friend.

"Thank you for sending me the owl back. Someone very special gave it to me, and I would have been sad not to have it anymore. When I was your age, I took a roll of quarters from the counter of a convenience store. My mom found it when I got home, and I got in so much trouble! I talked to your mom and dad, and I'm glad you didn't get in trouble and took responsibility for what you did. I understand wanting to take things that aren't yours, and I am glad you learned that even though you want to, it is the wrong thing to do."

Myles learned not to steal. He also learned that he was normal. He learned that he would be forgiven when he took responsibility for his actions. And (while I can't be sure) I don't think he ever stole any-thing again. The life lesson was lesson enough, as it was supported by empowered conversation, empathy, and clear boundaries rooted in our shared values.

~

Communication is learned behavior rooted in the way that we learn language. We've got the language part down. But learning how to communicate for connection? That's a conundrum for many of us.

If you start to pay attention, what you'll notice is that most people are having a conversation that is 80% with themselves and 20% with the other party to the conversation. We half listen, either constructing a response to what we think we are hearing, interpreting what we hear through our judgments, or going through our to-do list in our heads.

When we wholeheartedly claim that it is absolutely possible to parent without yelling, punishing, threatening, begging, or pleading, it isn't because we are abdicating our responsibility as parents to teach children to follow rules, act appropriately, and make decisions based on the values that we teach them. It is because we replace these parenting strategies with effective communication.

Communication becomes our core parenting strategy. With patience, consistency, and the willingness to hear our children, we have the opportunity to experience an entirely new paradigm of parenting.

The challenge to overcome is that most of us haven't been taught or modeled effective communication. Effective communication is a learnable skill that will serve you far beyond your role as a parent. Great communicators are great leaders, great partners, and great friends.

Chris's mother grew up in a house where feelings weren't welcome. Explicitly. So while Chris was determined to honor her kids in a way her mother hadn't honored her—as a complete and whole human being who mattered—she brought shame, guilt, and fear of open communication into motherhood. She desperately wanted to foster a feeling of openness in her family, but she couldn't model it with her kids. She held a lot of her feelings and experiences inside, simply putting her head down and pushing through whatever hardships she endured. And so her kids learned to do the same.

What we model is ultimately what our kids learn. Chris's mother modeled kindness but was not equipped to model expressing her feelings or having difficult conversations. Chris learned that she should best avoid them.

So that is what Chris learned. She grew up having flight and freeze reactions to difficult conversations, and when she misbehaved, which was not often, the punishment was quick and severe. She once lost sleepover privileges because she kept "budding in" to her older sister's playtime with a friend. At age nine, she hadn't yet learned to express her need to feel included, so she inserted herself despite repeated warnings. And she was punished—for months.

There was no curiosity about the why, only a reaction to the what. Peaceful Parenting embraces the "why." The "what" is what grows from the "why." Without seeking to uncover the why, parents are missing an important opportunity to allow their children to feel seen, heard, and understood, as well as the opportunity to model how to be curious about other people's "whys," including those of their future children.

Words are so powerful. They can hurt, and they can heal. They can create disconnection, and they can create separation. Becoming mindful of what we communicate and how we communicate creates a radical shift in our relationships. As we become more aware of our words and underlying emotional state when talking to others, we can become the living, breathing embodiment of our values. There's an old expression, "walk your talk." What if, instead, we thought about "talking our walk?" This means giving voice to our innermost selves and allowing others (including children) the space to do the same.

One of the key elements of effective communication is trust. Do we trust ourselves to speak our truth without being attached to how it is received? Can others trust us to share their truth without judgment or harsh reaction? This is why the early focus of this book has been on inner healing and personal growth.

We can all think back to our childhood experience of being stung by words from our parents, teachers, and friends. There is still a belief that harsh treatment is something kids need to experience to toughen them up for the cruelness of the world. But these experiences actually teach them to put up defenses and create filters between their inner experience and what they allow others to see to avoid pain.

As we heal and learn to communicate more effectively, we can learn a profound truth: That when we know who we are, love ourselves, and are anchored by our values and integrity, we are far less susceptible to words being able to cause us pain, manipulate us, or be used as weapons to cause us harm.

Our children's path to maturity will be far better served by receiving something that looks and sounds different than tough love. When we practice ways of communicating that lift, empower, encourage, and guide, we allow our children to find their voice, secured with a strong sense of self-worth and conviction.

We learned to communicate, as children, by being communicated to by our parents, caregivers, teachers, and eventually our friends and peers. So just as we've unconsciously passed down emotional wounding from one generation to the next, we've also inherited what are, most likely, some ineffective communication patterns and strategies.

Speaking and communication are habitualized over a lifetime and, of course, are influenced by how others spoke to us (and listened to us). If, as a child, we were taught that our voice was not valued, it can be challenging to ask for what we want as an adult. If our parents yelled a lot in our childhood home, we might reactively yell no matter how many times we promise ourselves we won't.

Like all habituated behavior, we can learn and practice a new way of communicating. Before we dive into the empowered communication framework, let's set some foundational practices.

ACTIVE LISTENING

For most of us, one of the hardest things to do is listen intently to another person when talking. Active listening is different from hearing. We can hear the sounds of another person's words without really listening to them with our full presence and attention. Of course, we all know exactly what it feels like to speak to someone and know that they aren't really listening. But can we also acknowledge that we do this like... all of the time?

Active listening is difficult because we all struggle with presence. Presence is the ability to be 100% in the moment, focused on what we see, feel, hear, taste and touch. We can't be present if we are distracted by our thoughts or stimulation (iPhone anyone?) that takes our attention away from our intention.

When having important conversations, because they are with someone who matters to us, whom we are committed to working with to solve problems and growing together, there is no greater gift we can give than actively listening with our full attention and presence.

We communicate with so much more than just our words. We communicate through micro-expressions on our faces, body language, and our inner emotions. When you're really listening to a person, for example, who is putting a happy face on top of their grief, you'll become aware that there's more going on than meets the ears.

When you choose to be available to someone with your active listening ears on, you have the opportunity to practice listening with all of your senses. You may find yourself wandering off into your own thoughts or forming a response before the other person finishes talking. Distraction is normal and expected. Go easy on yourself and just bring yourself back to listening. And be realistic. There are saints among us who can truly listen to every person with whom they communicate. I am not one of them. But for most of us, this is a tool we want to deploy for the people and situations that matter to us, and most importantly, for our work here as parents, for our children.

How to be an active listener for your child:

1. Slow down, show up, and listen intently

This won't happen perfectly or all of the time. Do your best each day to approach your interactions with your children with a clear intent to show up, slow down, and listen to their voices with your full attention. What if, every day, you could stop what you're doing, get to eye level with your child, and listen with so much presence you feel like your heart is going to explode? This is what presence feels like!

2. Refrain from interrupting

Accept imperfection, and take a noticing approach. How often do you interrupt your children? Their brains move so much more slowly than yours. They take more time to process their thoughts, memories, and desires. Can you listen to your children's natural processing without interrupting them and taking control of the conversation?

We teach our children by modeling. Are you modeling undivided attention? When your children tell you their feelings, stories, and fears, can you listen and do nothing but hear them without trying to solve their problems, rush their communication, or insert your worldview into their experience?

3. Refrain from comparison

Notice when you are comparing your child to someone else. Maybe this is their sibling, cousin, or friend. Can you show up and unconditionally accept your child as their unique self, more unique than a fingerprint or a snowflake, and stop comparing?

AVOIDING LABELS AND INTERPRETATION

Lina was known as the "happy child" in her family.

She is the youngest of three and, by her own account, most loved by her mom. In her family, she was "*the happy-go-lucky one, the one who keeps the peace,* and *the one who doesn't have a care in the world.*" She was always described as caring, thoughtful, considerate, and sensitive.

In her late twenties, Lina's relationship ended with the man she thought she would marry. She still lived at home because, in Singapore, the cultural expectation is that you live with your parents until marriage. She found herself struggling with what she now recognizes as undiagnosed depression.

Lina would go into the bathroom for privacy, turn the shower on, sit on the floor naked, and cry. Her mom would come to the door and ask, "What's going on?" Lina would tell her that everything was fine and that she was just taking a long shower, to which her mom would reply, "You're wasting water!"

One day during a conversation, Lina's mom took her hand, stroked it, and asked her, "Is everything ok? Do you have any worries that you want to tell me about?" Lina recognized that while it was thoughtful of her mom to reach out to her like that, she didn't feel she could trust her mom enough to be real about how she was feeling. It defied the person

Lina was supposed to be in her family, and she couldn't trust that her vulnerability would meet her with openness and empathy.

Lina didn't feel free to be anything but o.k. As 'the happy one,' Lina was also the child whose job was to essentially be a parent to her parents. She felt responsible for their feelings. Her past experiences in her family gave her pause to share her truth. She kept her heartbreak to herself.

Our understanding of the people who matter most to us in our lives will transform when we learn to listen openly. Relationships will deepen. Any stories about not being heard or being misunderstood will heal.

Can you listen to your child as they tell a story, ask a question, or receive their thoughts and fears without labeling them? When you have labels arise in your mind, thoughts like "Why does this kid have to be so obnoxious and loud?" or, "He never tells the truth; he's not honest." Judgments and labels are normal: They are deeply conditioned within us as we perceive our children. But they are rarely useful in creating intimate and honest relationships with our children.

As we become more aware of how we show up as listeners and interpreters, we offer a clear avenue toward direct, compassionate, and open conversations. Our words become less clouded by our projections and assumptions, and we can hear beyond behavior.

EMPOWERED COMMUNICATION

In Peaceful Parenting, we do the work of becoming the adult our child trusts, respects, and feels safest with, which means we are often the recipient of their big emotions, boundary-testing behaviors, and reactivity. This is where the PEACE process comes in!

Before we dive into this life-changing process, let's explore behaviors a bit more carefully. Remember, all behavior, positive or negative, is an expression of a need and whether that need is met or unmet. When we witness unacceptable, negative, or harmful behavior from our child, our instinct is to react in any way that will get them to change or stop what they are doing.

We can access so much more empathy when we look at our child's behavior through the analogy of a plant and its roots. The plant is what we see. It's the behavior the child is exhibiting. But underneath that behavior are the roots: the complex, interwoven web that is comprised of:

- Feelings
- Emotional needs
- Physiological needs
- Thoughts
- Beliefs
- Context of situation
- Brain development/neurological capacity
- Nervous system regulation
- Quality of secure attachment

People often ask us if Peaceful Parenting works for neurodiverse children, and this is the perfect place to answer this question as it provides a lot of clarity. A child on the spectrum for autism may never have the capacity to control her energetic body. A child who suffers a physical limitation may never be able to participate in household chores, even though we have a family value of contribution. We are parent-centric, meaning that we desire to give you, the parent, the ability to meet the child you have with the tools to embrace, accept, and unconditionally love them beyond their behaviors.

Getting curious about your child's worldview and taking a moment to pause and see the situation through their eyes gives us much more insight into the roots that underlie the behavior. Instead of creating conflict, resentment, and frustration, we can meet our child right where they are, with compassion and connection, while giving them the tools to learn appropriate behavior, sound decision-making, and morality.

What is the PEACE Process?

The PEACE Process is a five-step framework to replace traditional ideas of discipline and punishment related to power-over or power-under parenting.

With the PEACE Process, our world no longer needs damaging strategies to achieve harmony in a home. There is no longer a need for:

- → Threats to control a child's behavior
- → Fear-based obedience
- → Manipulation via bribes or rewards for desired behavior
- → Spanking, pinching, swatting, slapping
- → Punitive consequences to teach the child a lesson
- → Parenting from fear
- → Parenting with helplessness and despair
- → Timeouts or shame corners
- → Power struggles out of desperation
- → Lying and secrets

Why the PEACE Process?

We use the PEACE process as our main plan of action or response map in any given parenting scenario because we value:

- → Connection over correction
- → Relationship longevity over immediate gratification
- → Equality and mutual respect
- → Communication over coercion
- → Collaboration over "a parent knows best"

When do we use the PEACE Process?

As a parent, grandparent, or child-care provider, you can use the PEACE Process in every parent-child scenario. Yes, everyone!

We all need a framework for HOW to respond to challenging moments like:

→ Sibling squabbles
→ Child not following through with an agreement
→ Child struggling to honor the family boundaries
→ Behavior from the child (or parent!) that results in harm of any kind
→ The family struggling to work as a team
→ Parent and child disagreeing and getting stuck in power struggle
→ Conflict resolution

How does the PEACE Process work?

The PEACE Process includes five intentional phases. You can use them individually in any given parenting scenario where a response is necessary, or the PEACE Process can be used in its entirety. This formula is rooted in all Ten Pillars of Peaceful Parenting and breathes life into what you have learned thus far. This is how we *do* Peaceful Parenting!

The PEACE process becomes the foundation of our parenting. We teach our values, establish and maintain agreed-upon boundaries and limits, and create new agreements as children grow.

Let's go step-by-step through this revolutionary process.

Remember as you go: Get comfortable, anchor yourself into inner safety, and engage in an expansive belief like, "Anything is possible" or "I am capable of learning new things."

THE FIVE-STEP PROCESS FOR RESPONDING TO ANY PARENTING SCENARIO:

→ Presence
→ Empathy
→ Acknowledge what is true
→ Conscious communication
→ Explore solutions together

Let's work through each of the five steps below.

STEP ONE: Presence

We live in a disconnected world where it's easy to become disconnected from ourselves. Most of us spend most of the time in a reverie of our thoughts, feelings, and distractions.

The practice (and it is a practice!) of PRESENCE allows us to be with our children FULLY, so we can meet them in the now and create new ways of relating, problem-solving, and cooperation.

Before responding to ANY parenting situation, take as little as three seconds (if the response requires immediate attention) to ground into your anchor. Get as present as possible. You could easily escalate the entire scenario when you approach a parenting scenario NOT fully present, rooted in your body and internal safety.

You can tell your child, "I am coming to help you, but I need to get a drink of water first." Suppose that is impossible because an IMMEDIATE response is required, say in instances of threatened safety or real danger. In that case, you can tell your child, *"I am not fully present to help you at this moment, but I am going to work on becoming present while I'm here."*

You aren't going to be perfectly present every time you are needed to respond in your parenting. You don't have to model perfection; you get to model the process. You get to show your child, *"even though I struggle getting present sometimes, I am still committed to my process."*

STEP TWO: Empathy and emotional connection

After establishing presence, we connect our right brain to our child's right brain. We get to connect to feelings and needs. We do not need to FIX, CHANGE, or SAVE our children from their feelings, conflicts, or growth opportunities. From presence and inner safety, we can simply BE with our children and ourselves in our emotions, feelings, and needs.

Practice the FEEL framework.

We can name and identify feelings and needs without jumping into solutions. "Feel it to heal it" and "name it to tame it."

There are so many benefits of cultivating empathy in your relationships. When you can give and receive empathy, each person you show up for feels a deep sense of being heard. When someone knows we hear them, defensiveness eases, and connection becomes possible.

Empathy contributes to healthy differentiation, as well as emotional security. With empathy, you can be a true companion and support another person without taking on their struggles as your own. However, when we mistakenly use methods of communication that do not come from a place of true empathy, we miss an opportunity to see, hear, and understand the other person in their experience.

What Is Not Empathy?

The following responses are what many mistakenly offer to someone's expression of emotion or difficulty. But they gloss over the other person's lived experience. Ideally, we can practice being conscious of the following habitual responses. Instead of our habituated response, we can ask the speaker how they would like to be supported when they share something with us.

SYMPATHY: Bring attention back to yourself. *"Oh, I am so sorry. I feel terrible for you."* This may meet the need for caring, but it isn't true empathy.	**ADVICE:** You assume the other person wants to know what you think they should do. *"Well, what you could do is . . ."* This may meet your need to support after empathy is received.
EXPLAIN/ANALYZE: You believe that if you tell someone why they feel the way they do, they will feel better. *"You just feel bad because . . ."* This may meet a need for clarity after the need for empathy is met.	**CORRECT:** You try to point out someone's mistake in interpreting. *"He didn't do that to hurt you. It was an accident."* This may meet a need for groundedness after the need for empathy is met.
CONSOLE: *"It will be okay. You're okay. Everything will work out."* This may meet a need for emotional regulation.	**TELL A STORY:** *"The same thing happened to me. This one time . . ."* This may meet a need for acceptance or belonging.
PUSH AWAY FEELINGS: You might be uncomfortable, so you tell others not to feel what they feel. *"Come on, smile. Don't be sad."* *"Just calm down and take a deep breath."* *"It's not that big of a deal. Just let it go."* This typically does not meet any needs.	**INVESTIGATE/INTERROGATE:** *"Why did you do that? What made you feel that way?"* This may meet a need for clarity after the need for empathy is met. Still, this is typically about the listener's need for clarity and information and arises from anxiety. Questioning *why* a person did something puts them on the defensive.

EVALUATE: You decide if another's emotional response is appropriate or not. *"You are overreacting. This is no big deal."* This typically doesn't meet any needs. All emotional responses are inherently valid because they are part of the human experience.	**EDUCATE:** *"What I see about the situation is . . . The reason you feel like that is . . ."* This may meet a need for learning and support after the need for empathy is met.
ONE-UP: *"That's awful, but something worse happened to me, and I was devastated."* This typically doesn't meet any needs.	**DIAGNOSE:** *"Sounds like you just need more sleep. Let's have you go to bed early tonight."* This may meet a need for learning and support if it is consent-based and offered after the need for empathy is met.
DEMAND: *"If you don't get control of your emotions, I'm leaving!"* This typically doesn't meet any needs.	**DENIAL OF CHOICE:** *"It's hard, but we all have to do it."* This typically doesn't meet any needs.
NOD & SMILE: You feel uncomfortable and just want to get out of the situation. Or you lose track of yourself and become completely lost in the other person's experience. This typically doesn't meet any needs.	**COLLUSION:** You agree and add to judgments and blame. *"You're right. He is a jerk!"* This may meet a need for support or to be seen/heard in the moment but then escalates or entrenches reactivity.
SILVER LINING: Move past what's happening toward some possible positive outcome. *"You will learn so much from this experience!"; "That person wasn't a good friend for you anyway."* This may meet a need for encouragement or hope after the need for empathy is met.	**CHEERLEADING:** You assume the need is for hope or reassurance. *"You're a strong person. You can get through this."; "You've been through worse and made it."; "I believe in you."* This may meet a need for encouragement or hope after the need for empathy is met.

Genuine empathy doesn't need to say much at all. Empathy is accessed when we allow another person's lived experience into our awareness. It is an acknowledgment of their feelings, circumstances, and environment. It is best acknowledged through reflection.

"I hear your words." "I feel your sadness." "I see your frustration."

Empathy is about so much more than simply saying these words. It's about meaning it. We can tell when people give lip service to our brave willingness to share our vulnerability, messiness, or failures. And so we must acknowledge that when we do this to our kids, they can feel it too.

STEP THREE: Acknowledge what is true

From presence and right-brain connection, next we connect to the left brain. We get to ignite our thinking brain and practice mindsight in both ourselves and in service to our child.

Acknowledge what is true in your emotional, physical, and mental body.

Part of giving empathy to yourself is being candid about your feelings at that moment. They may not be those thoughts or feelings you want to act on, like, "This kid is driving me crazy! I just want to leave!"

** Don't edit these thoughts or feelings. It's important to acknowledge them, no matter the situation.

** If you judge or try to suppress your thoughts or feelings, they could emerge later, possibly in not the healthiest ways.

Telling yourself, "I shouldn't be this angry," makes your emotion STRONGER! What we resist persists and strengthens.

Separate your feelings from your interpretations.

On the next page, you will find a list of words we often mistakenly identify as feelings when they are actually interpretations.

For example, if someone forgets your birthday, you could say that you felt unloved, when your true feelings may have been anger, sadness, or even disappointment. But to say that you felt unloved assumes the other person's feelings behind that action: not loving you. This language can often trigger defensiveness in the listener and avoid a genuine feeling, becoming more of a mental projection.

Whether these interpretations are accurate or inaccurate, continuing to use this language can blur the distinctions between feelings and interpretations. This habit can remove us from genuine empathy and lead us to emotionally fueled assumptions. We draw highly inaccurate conclusions, often projections of our unmet underlying needs.

Interpretations often:

→ Have an "un" or "mis" at the beginning or an "ed" at the end
→ Require the action of someone else
→ Trigger defensiveness in your listener

Behind each of these words are precious feelings and needs.

YOUR TASK: Circle three words you've used recently and name the feelings and needs present for you when you used each word.

Abandoned	Provoked	Put down
Belittled	Smothered	Taken advantage of
Confined	Trampled	Coerced
Discounted	Unloved	Disrespected
Harassed	Used	Insulted
Intimidated	Left out	Invisible
Judged	Bullied	Manipulated
Neglected	Overpowered	Patronized

Rejected	Interrupted	Wronged
Unappreciated	Isolated	Victimized
Unsupported	Misunderstood	Tricked
Violated	Pressured	Unseen
Attacked	Threatened	Alienated
Criticized	Unheard	Blamed
Dumped on	Unwanted	

Make neutral observations vs. evaluations:

Observations:

Name only what you see and hear objectively, as if through the lens of a video recorder or a sportscaster.

- → "I see your clothes are on the floor."
- → "You are on your phone past our agreed-upon time."
- → "I found your shoes in the yard."

Evaluations, interpretations, and criticism:

These are statements made with a thick filter. They typically support the belief that *"my child is doing this TO ME"* and have the child believe that *"my parent is doing this TO ME."* It's inherently separating.

- → *"You are so messy and disorganized. I wish you would clean your room for once in your life."*
- → *"You're being so disrespectful right now. Give that phone to me. I give an inch, and you take a mile."*
- → *"I found your shoes outside AGAIN. Why can't you simply pick up your shoes and bring them inside?"*

Remember, your role as a Peaceful Parent is to look UNDER your child's behavior.

What is true is that your child's behavior and capacity for conflict resolution is an expression of several things: The state of their nervous system, the quality of security within their attachment to you as their care provider, their brain development, their emotional intelligence, and their capacity to communicate while stressed.

STEP FOUR: Conscious communication

"When your internal dialogue is centered in a language of life, you will be able to focus your attention on the actions you could take to manifest a situation that meets your needs along with those of others." - Dr. Marshall B. Rosenberg, Ph.D.

In the PEACE Process, we mindfully name and consciously communicate:

→ Our feelings and needs with clarity and self-responsibility.

→ The child's feelings and needs with empathy (remember, this comes AFTER safety has been established and the communication brain is back "online").

→ What is true about the current circumstances based on an objective viewpoint?

→ The need to give space to each child to tell their version of the story; to allow each child a chance to be fully heard and understood.

→ The importance of reflecting back on what you hear your child saying and asking clarifying questions without judgment. We want to model how to speak from self-responsibility and how to make neutral observations instead of interpretations.

When we communicate consciously, we share what is true within our experience without blaming, shaming, or guilting others for that experience. So after we acknowledge what we observe, we can share our feelings and perceptions about the situation:

"I am feeling sad."

"I notice tightness in my chest. I am scared."

"I am angry."

As Peaceful Parents, it's o.k. to show our emotions to our kids! Especially as we develop the capacity to do so without making them anyone else's responsibility. This is the opposite of gaslighting. We take full responsibility for our feelings, needs, and values and communicate them clearly and peacefully to our children.

We will go further into conflict resolution and repair in the next chapter, but for now, try this simple communication framework the next time you need to address inappropriate behavior, breaking the rules, or ignoring boundaries.

1. State your feelings: "I am feeling _____."
2. Use clear observation to share why: "I see that you _____."
3. State the agreement, boundary, or rule: "We agreed as a family that [Insert family value]
4. Tell me what is happening for you:

Next, we shift into addressing the situation at hand by naming and facilitating mutually beneficial outcomes for all parties involved.

STEP FIVE: Exploring solutions together

These are the concrete actions you'd like family members to take. Invite your child to explore a solution TOGETHER with you. Collaboration is the goal so we can maintain social engagement within the relationship. Any behavior correction approach (threats, bribes, punishments, rewards) risks pushing the child into their fight (aggression), flight (shut down or freeze), or fawn (pleasing others against their true needs and desires) responses.

These solutions are rooted in:

→ Shared and previously agreed-upon family values
→ A belief that everyone's needs in the family are equal
→ A belief that anything is possible
→ A belief that the parent is a safe space and here to guide the child through conflict with capability

These solutions are:

→ Reminders of what the family values most
→ Flexible when possible, non-negotiable when safety is concerned
→ Consistent without rigidity
→ NOT stuck on strategies (See below)

Exploring solutions with children under 7:

The parent may have the solution in mind and facilitates the child to find their way to a solution on their own. They stand sturdy in the family value while supporting the child through their resistance or rejection of the boundary or solution.

Examples:

"I would love to see us working together as a team here. How do you think we could make this happen? We could play outside on the trampoline or nestle in for some book reading."

Meeting potential objections:

Child:

→ *"I don't want to do either of those! I don't want to work as a team!"*

Parent:

→ *"Ok."* (Silence, presence. Maybe a hug, or getting low to the ground.) *"Sounds like you may not be ready to work as a team right now. Let's relax here for a bit until your body feels ready enough. Take your time. I'm here as your safe place. (Pause) I am ready to help you work as a team when you are."*

OR

→ *"We need to get this playroom tidied up before dinner. I'm really glad we were able to hear each other. Suz, what would you like to clean up, the dolls or the blocks? Lily, would you like to help Daddy tidy up the cars or the play kitchen?"*

Meeting potential objections:

Suz:

"NO! I hate cleaning up blocks. I always clean up the blocks, and Lily gets to do whatever she wants!"

Parent:

"Mmmm." (Soft face, soft gaze, warm tone) *"It's hard to feel stuck in one job. It sounds like you'd like something new and different. How about . . . (silence) . . . hmmm . . . do you have any ideas? I believe we can work this out in a way that feels right for you."*

This allows our child to be a part of the process while remaining rooted in the safety and sturdiness of our support and compassion.

Exploring solutions for children between 7 and 12:

Ideally, the family has clear values that the child has witnessed being modeled for years. The parent is still the compassionate leader, with much more spaciousness regarding how the family value is honored. The boundaries and solutions are more flexible and creative. The parent can present more than two options at a time and invite the child to expand upon the options. The parent remains the "safe space" and will inform the child if their proposed solution misaligns with family values or does not consider the entire family's needs. Remember, their brain is still learning to create solutions involving extensive thought and understanding of natural consequences.

Note: If family values are just being introduced and the child was previously parented with power-over strategies, they may be in the 0-7 solution process category.

Examples:

Parent:

→ *"It sounds like you two need to come to an agreement around this."*

OR

→ *"It sounds like we need to find a solution to this problem together. Remember our family values of integrity and communication. I trust you to be creative, and I'll be here to facilitate."*

Exploring solutions for children 13 and older:

Children come into their values at this age and may sway between embracing the family values and rebelling against them. Even with the most secure attachments, children of this age are exploring whether they agree with family values.

Note: If family values are just being introduced, they may be more in the phase of the 0- to 7-year-old, who needs very grounded and supportive modeling from the parent, with only a couple of choices that work well for the whole family.

Examples:

Parent:

→ *"I am deeply longing for your safety. I am super uncomfortable when you don't answer your phone after dark. My idea of a solution is for you to be home before dark while we work on an agreement we both trust will work for us. What's your idea?"*

Child:

→ *"I honestly forget to turn my ringer up. I promise I'm safe. My idea is that before I leave the house, we make sure my ringer is up as loud as possible."*

Parent:

→ *"I am willing to try that once, and if you do not answer your phone after that idea, then we need to re-work this."*

Child:

→ *"Okay, that sounds good to me."*

Establishing Boundaries or Limits from Family Values Using the PEACE Process

The whole energy around establishing boundaries is to connect and cooperate **with** your child. We're not enforcing anything; we are providing a **structure**.

We trust that our children will learn our family limits over time, with lots and lots of practice and empathy. Your child may not like the boundary or limit you set and will need to release feelings. Your job is to be the emotional coach, to be present, and support your child with empathy. This does not mean changing your boundary if you are confident, clear, and secure in its expression, especially regarding your child's safety.

You can shift HOW you're going to HONOR this boundary, but not the actual boundary.

Example: The boundary is "Our family eats dinner together every weeknight."

The value it's rooted in: Connection

The possible strategies to honor this value and uphold the boundary:

→ Dinner on a picnic blanket in the living room.
→ Eating around the table while one person reads aloud a story to keep young children's attention.
→ Young children can stand and move around during dinner in order to tend to their sensory needs and stay focused.
→ Dinner happens, and the child can choose to EAT, or they can choose to simply be in the room and wait to eat until their body says they are hungry.
→ The family eats at a time that works for everyone's hunger, not just the parents.
→ The family prioritizes NO evening activities or playdates, so the children are not too tired to engage in a family activity.

→ The parent ensures the meal consists of foods that appeal to the child while providing new options. (Many children who struggle with limited food options would greatly benefit from an occupational therapist; this is usually sensory-processing related.)

→ Dinner happens at the family table while some kids chat and some work on homework.

See how this works? As adults, we want to show our children that our boundaries are precious, even sacred, AND that we are not stuck on the strategy as to how this boundary occurs. We are willing to be flexible and creative.

As the adult, you may believe **you** should determine how a boundary is followed, especially if you were not allowed to participate in negotiations or collaboration around family boundaries and limits as a kid.

The value **beneath** the boundary or limit is the reason **why** you are committed to this boundary and committed to the negotiation process. Children need to feel safe and protected as they grow. And they need to feel that they have the container of safety.

Clear boundaries create an environment of support around a child within which they can explore and engage with themself, others, and the world.

Your environment of support includes:

→ Daily routines
→ Supportive belief systems
→ Clear boundaries according to family values
→ Conscious and connected communication

What are boundaries? Boundaries are:

→ Consciously planned with family values in mind.

→ Consciously established with an understanding of developmentally appropriate expectations of a child's mental, physical, and spiritual development.

PERMANENT VERSUS EVOLVING BOUNDARIES

Many parents struggle to understand when to negotiate the boundary and when to stand firm. Often, the easiest way to navigate this is to ask: "Will I always feel this way, or might my feelings change over time?"

If the feeling is very clearly going to remain static over time, it is a **permanent boundary**. There is usually a lot of clarity for the adult in these boundaries.

Examples: "Under no circumstances will my child ever be able to use illegal substances in my home." Or, *"A child causing physical harm to someone else is never acceptable."*

When an adult lovingly sets these limits, the child may have big feelings about them. In this instance, the adult can hold space for their feelings, help the child feel heard and seen, and collaboratively discuss alternatives with the child. The collaboration isn't in the boundary but rather in the workable and mutually agreeable alternatives, whatever they may be.

Conversely, an **evolving boundary** is likely to change over time. **Most** parenting boundaries evolve.

Examples: "My child is too young to go to the playground without an adult, but they will be able to go with just their friends when they're older." Or, *"My child can't set their own bedtime yet, but when they're [x years old], I'll offer them more flexibility as long as they get enough rest overall."*

When an adult lovingly sets these limits, we can say: *"This is our plan for now."* It's not intended to be permanent, yet we can have respectful firmness in the boundary given the current situation.

Often, the adult might hold space for the child's perspective by saying something like: "I hear how much you want x. For now, this is our plan. I will let you know if and when we can revisit it." At this point, as with the permanent boundary, the adult can validate feelings and collaborate about alternatives. The adult may also offer some flexibility within the boundary, if appropriate.

For example, the adult might still have a set bedtime for the child but is willing to make exceptions for certain occasions to see how it goes. This doesn't make the adult wishy-washy. On the contrary, it makes us flexible and reinforces the benefits of exploring caregiving through a lens of curiosity.

And, of course, if the child raises a perspective that the adult hadn't considered and seems like a reasonable solution, it models flexibility to say, "You know what? I hadn't thought of it that way. Thank you. Let's try that and see how it goes." Some boundaries can evolve in the moment and show the child that the adult values their input. It helps the child feel seen, even if it's not a permanent alteration to the boundary.

Finally, it's important to note that if the child is very young, stating that the boundary might be flexible "someday" could be confusing, disconcerting, and/or frustrating. With young children, simple and direct answers are usually best.

Evolving boundaries allow adults to feel less rigidity in their parenting. Less rigidity naturally lends itself to fewer power struggles over time. Leading with confidence, for both permanent and evolving boundaries, is beneficial regardless of the child's age.

HOW TO NAVIGATE NATURAL AND
LOGICAL CONSEQUENCES

Conscious parenting is not parenting devoid of consequences. Rather, it's devoid of arbitrary and unilaterally adult-imposed consequences (punishments or loss of privileges).

With **natural consequences**, the adult (within safety limits) allows the child to learn through their experience, even if the outcome is undesirable. The result of the action is the "teacher" that helps the child understand the results of their actions (or lack thereof).

Example: A child refuses to study for an upcoming test because they're too busy chatting online with friends. Rather than force the studying or grounding the child and making them cease social contact, for the time being, the adult allows the child to get a less-than-stellar grade on the test. After the grade is received, we can work with our child to find the root cause of their lack of interest in studying. Is the material too boring or too hard? Is the child lonely and needing social contact to help them feel "seen?" Is the child being bullied? Something else? The adult gets curious rather than punishing and further alienating the child.

A natural consequence is usually the most effective teacher. Natural consequences work particularly well if the adult is lovingly supportive of the child as they process the ramifications of their choices and decisions. The adult refrains from blaming and shaming and works with the child to guide them forward.

With **logical consequences**, the adult does "direct" the outcome, albeit not in a punitive way.

Example: A child wants to ride their bike without a helmet. If the adult feels a helmet is important and non-negotiable, the adult may set a boundary and require the helmet to ride the bike. If the child goes biking without the helmet anyway, the adult might then remove access to the bike.

Unlike a threat or a punishment, the adult describes the consequence with loving kindness, making sure to hear the child's perspective. Once again, the adult approaches the situation from a state of curiosity. In this example, is the child's helmet uncomfortable? Too hot? Is the chin strap too tight? Perhaps there's an easy solution.

With natural and logical consequences, the adult supports the child through empowered communication, as life teaches the child its most valuable lessons.

Access our FREE five-part training on the Peace Process at www.jai-instituteforparenting.com/book-resources

INVITATION TO PRACTICE

- Reflect on a recent conflict that did not play out as you hoped (noting the use of any punitive or arbitrary consequences). Rewrite your ideal version of the scenario, identifying one or two areas where you could have supported yourself or your child more effectively.
- When you anticipate using the PEACE process, plan your preparation for each step.
- Celebrate ANY success in any stage of the PEACE process.
- Incorporate your family values into your daily life: post them around your home, have frequent conversations about them, and invite your family members to reflect on how they are modeling the values.
- Make a plan to revisit your family values as your children grow and your priorities shift.
- Keep practicing the PEACE Process, even when it seems unsuccessful. Practicing and reflecting strengthen your skills.

ADAM, AGE 12

How are you aware that the way you've been parented is different than your peers?

Just by talking with them, I know their parents are different.

What is the biggest difference this has made in your relationship with your parents or your life?

It's always been this way, so I don't feel any different. I have a good relationship with my parents.

What's been good about it?

We can talk about anything. I don't feel like my parents will punish me for any mistakes I make, and there are no threats of taking things away. We get to actually talk about things.

What would you want parents who are thinking about not using punishments or consequences with their kids to know?

You have to have consequences for your actions enough for them to remember it, but not enough to scar them. You don't want to have to beat it into them so they can remember and not do it again.

What differences do you notice between the relationship you have with your parent(s) and the relationship of your friends who were parented more traditionally with their parents?

They are less social and almost expect bad things to happen with their parents when they do stuff.

CHAPTER NINE

Anger, Aggression, and Rage, Oh My

Our most shameful parenting moments are usually born of anger.

Several years ago, I'd just returned from a trip where I had the lovely experience of staying in an Airbnb with bedbugs. It was a rough time in my life. I was recently divorced and less than a year out from grieving the loss of my best friend to ovarian cancer.

I was a hot mess.

I took all the clothes from the trip and double-bagged them in garbage bags, which I put in the garage. One of the bags held clothes that were my best friend's. One of the t-shirts in the bags even still smelled like her. I hadn't ever washed it.

It was one of my kids' jobs to take out the trash, which they responsibly did. (Can you see where this is going?)

As I walked into the garage and realized the bags were not there, I instantly knew what had happened and broke into sobs. I called the kids down and started screaming at them. "Where did the bag go? The one with my clothes!"

"Mom," my then-ten-year-old son said quietly (they were already terrified), "I thought it was trash. I took it out to the curb this morning."

I laid into them with the mother of all hysterical guilt trips, culminating with throwing myself on the stairs in dramatic fashion and breaking down completely. My rage was making a mess and scaring the bejesus out of my kids.

I wish I could say that was the only time something like this happened, but it's not. There was the time my ex-husband showed up unexpectedly at an event I was at with the kids, and I left in anger, leaving them feeling abandoned. There was the time I yelled at my son, who was having a panic attack, to pull it together.

I'm not proud to share these things, but I hope to normalize our worst moments and give you hope that we don't need to be the victim of or make our children the victim of our anger. When we keep our worst moments locked behind closed doors, we make our children complicit in the secret truth of our worst proclivities.

We slam doors.

We yell in their faces.

We take away their favorite toy or don't let them go to their friend's house.

We call them names.

We shame them.

We tell them we are leaving or demand that they leave, seething disdainfully.

And then we feel shame. Deep, potent, crumbling shame. And so do they.

❃

Anger is the six-pack abs of parent coaching. Meaning it's the thing that most people want to resolve immediately. Anger is complex. It has so many tendrils and defenses. It hides underneath the surface, where it bubbles and brews, like a steaming tea kettle, until the pressure becomes too great, and the lid blows off.

One of our coaches shared a story of working with a client who hired her specifically because she wanted to control her anger. Wanting to give this mom what she came for, she jumped right into this piece of our process. But the mom was so defensive. There was no access point to actual transformation. Every time the coach tried to offer tools, she touched a nerve. Without the prior work, she was met with justifications, "yeah, buts," and blaming others. She wisely returned to the beginning of the work, realizing there was more to be done.

Without the foundations of emotional awareness, defined values, and communication, we can't truly transform our relationship with and to anger because anger scares us. It can feel like an uncontrollable force. Anger turns us into people we hardly recognize and are embarrassed to acknowledge. Most of us were conditioned to control our anger, so we don't have a positive model for handling it.

Destini Davis, the Instagram superstar, was made for Peaceful Parenting. Because we know her heart so well and because she's a Jai Certified Parenting coach, I can tell you that the woman you see on social media is indeed the woman she is in real life.

Destini's anger made her a bad kid, a problem teenager, and an angry woman. As a child, her parents often conveyed that her anger was the worst part of herself. So she tamped it down. She learned to avoid it, quiet it, and repress it. Anger became such a scary thing that she became the consummate people pleaser.

One day, in her Jai practice group, she realized she was scared of her daughter's anger. She would bend over backward to keep her from getting upset and was inadvertently passing on the message: Anger is not something that we get to feel or experience.

In a powerful moment, she realized that she would need to make friends with her anger to support her daughter's healthy development.

Controlling and avoiding it weren't doing her or her child any favors. We don't typically address anger until we've done the earlier work of this book because, for most of us, our anger is so defended that there's no tip, trick, or strategy to deal with our anger the way we were taught. Remember the line in *Beauty and the Beast*, where Belle demands of the beast: "You MUST control your temper!"

It may have worked in a Disney cartoon, but in real life, controlling anger is as futile as controlling the wind. And so, we get to create a new, healthy, and empowered relationship with anger because anger is one of the most powerful tools of awareness, truth, and safety we have as human beings.

Actually, you must NOT control your temper

Repressed anger hurts us and others. When we don't acknowledge our anger, or we don't allow it in others, we are essentially trapping a toxic concoction of neurochemicals inside of our body. We rob ourselves of a vital component of our experiences from the past and in the present.

Resentments build. We become the very thing we hate to see in others. Bitter, resigned, and cynical. We start treating the people we love most poorly. We become overly critical of ourselves and others. We speak to our loved ones with contempt. We avoid conflict and shut down conversations. We make our anger other people's fault: "You made me (insert unhealthy expression of anger here)."

No wonder we don't want to feel our anger! We've been hurting others and being hurt by others through unhealthy expressions of anger for a really long time. Here's a hard truth to swallow: When we've been holding our anger in for a lifetime, our children are the easiest targets for its wrath. They are smaller than we are, can't abandon us, and won't fight back and win. Often, our safest and most reliable relationships receive the brunt of our anger.

Ashley has a lot to be angry about. She suffered abuse as a child and is the daughter of a narcissist. So growing up, she played the role of the consummate good girl. But her anger found an outlet when she got married—her husband. Unhealed, a lifetime of pain was doing a number on her marriage. She found someone she could unleash on, but at what cost to her family's health? She had to do the work and heal.

The journey toward Peaceful Parenting isn't about getting rid of our anger. It's about discovering new and healthy expressions of anger and teaching our children to do the same.

A word on yelling

Recent research shows that a child exposed to yelling is likely to experience more difficulty with aggression themselves, including lashing out physically or verbally. An eye-opening finding, shown to us by the *American Journal of Psychiatry* and Dr. Len Lantz, says that yelling has the same detrimental effects as spanking on a child's growing brain and body. This is echoed in the *Journal of Child Psychology and Psychiatry*,[2] which affirms yelling impacts the cortisol levels within a child's developing brain, impacting higher long-term risk for anxiety, depressive symptoms, and difficulty managing stress.

This evidence may not feel comfortable to read. Allowing ourselves to face the uncomfortable science that proves that yelling is a harmful communication strategy can fuel our resolve to dedicate ourselves to a new path. The path away from yelling and into self-accountability means taking care of our physiological and emotional needs, practicing clear communication, and dedicating ourselves to intention, prevention, and repair. Let's unpack this dynamic trio.

A very common "why" behind the yelling behavior is a parent living out a generational pattern of expressing their anger, frustration, and impatience through the voice. If we witnessed our caregiver resort to yelling in the midst of overwhelm, we have likely picked up this same habit.

In addition to replaying what we were modeled, the response you received as a child when *you* yelled creates an extra layer of association. In 1949, neuropsychologist Donald Hebb first used the phrase "what fires together, wires together" to describe how pathways in the brain are formed and reinforced through repetition. Think of it this way: How many of us remember being yelled at as a child to stop our stress-based behaviors? A yelling parent yelling at a yelling child to stop yelling. Talk about a crossfire!

A HEIGHTENED NERVOUS SYSTEM GONE HAYWIRE

Here's what's happening in simple terms: If we weren't consistently met with peace and gentleness as children, we most likely struggle to find self-connection and an internal sense of safety within our own intense emotions. We are, therefore, susceptible to outbursts of an overstimulated central nervous system.

Remember, the central nervous system **controls most functions of the body and mind**. It consists of two parts: the brain and the spinal cord. The body experiences our external environment and sends signals to the brain to let us know if we are experiencing safety or danger. If our body experiences overstimulation or interprets a stressful experience as actual danger, our brain then begins receiving signals to prepare for an attack.

Our aggression center takes over, and we go into the fight response. When the body floods with adrenaline and cortisol, we prepare for fight, flight, or freeze. We yell as a strategy to advocate and protect our unmet needs through an unconscious, instinctual stress response. We yell to express our 'fight' energy; it releases the stress built up in our nervous system.

Expressing through our vocal cords and voice is a human way of coping with internal stress and perceiving an external lack of control. And it causes harm if used consistently over time. This is why we sit and ask ourselves:

- *How can I soothe my brain and body before getting desperate?*
- *How can I keep centered despite the external chaos?*
- *When I yell, what needs am I trying to advocate for and protect?*
- *How can I communicate these needs in a safer, more effective way?*

THE POWER OF PREVENTION

Parents typically reach out for support once they feel like they have hit rock bottom. They seek the tools and strategies to help pick them up off the ground and begin untangling patterns. What if we took a more pro-active approach, examined the daily dynamics between ourselves and our children, and asked: *How can I get ahead of this the next time? How can unnecessary stress be eliminated?*

For example, a very common time for parents everywhere to yell is when it's time to leave the house in the morning. In an ideal world, everyone's shoes have a special space near the front door the night before. Ideally, everyone in the home knows that the cereal on top of the fridge is for the toddler only. Ideally, the dog stays in the kennel or backyard during the busy morning shuffle. Ideally, the parent gets up a few minutes early to take ten deep, long breaths and set an intention to mind their internal stress levels and commit to their calming sensory tools during the morning rush.

What if we created systems during our most yell-vulnerable times of day and proactively supported our internal stress levels? This can be a challenging space to navigate for many parents already experiencing burnout and a lack of reliable support systems. But the effort of strategizing and implementing preventative measures saves so much angst and frustration.

Leading a family with self-accountability and responsibility can feel like a burden for parents with low inner and outer resources. Brainstorming with a friend, partner, or parent coach is beneficial. Someone else's viewpoint can help us clarify our recurring pain points. We can start making practical changes to reduce yelling and create stress relief.

EMBRACING REALITY

While prevention can be our most effective ally, sometimes things simply go haywire, don't they? We can't avoid stress altogether. Surprises happen. Accommodations become necessary.

An intimate understanding of our own stress thermometer and calming sensory tools are key. Our ability to soothe or return our nervous system to social engagement and out of fight, flight, or freeze is known as self-regulation. When we can regulate our nervous system back to an internal state of safety, we are much more likely to be able to notice and name our feelings and needs, plus communicate our requests clearly and non-violently.

A father I was speaking with recently told me that he completely lost it at dinner time when his kids would not sit down and eat their food. They were wiggling and complaining and just could not focus! Before this dedicated dad knew it, he "flipped his lid" and regressed into "yelling dad" against his best intention to remain calm and respond with patience, trust, and empathy.

I asked him, "What happened? What built up within you that created the perfect storm of yelling and rage?"

He responded, "I was simply not paying attention to myself."

He was so focused on his kids and their stress, the multitasking bonanza of single parenting dinner prep, that he lost awareness of his internal state. He hadn't slept well the night before. Undoubtedly, he did not go from zero to a hundred in an instant. His stress thermometer was building over hours and hadn't been tended to along the way.

TRACKING YOUR THERMOMETER, LOWERING YOUR ANCHOR

Our commitment to self-awareness of our stress levels is key to preventing or softening our nervous system's need to express stress through our voice. We can visualize our internal stress levels as a thermometer. The bottom of the thermometer is our green zone. Our body feels loose, light, and able to adjust and adapt. Thinking is clear, and thoughts are optimistic.

Then we notice our stress levels rising into yellow. For the dad above, by working with a parent coach, he can now identify that his first stress signal is racing thoughts. His mind goes into "must get this all done right now!" mode. When we know our earliest stress signal(s), we can drop our anchor and begin regulating ourselves back to "green."

Our anchor is our connection to the present moment. This symbol, known typically as "a heavy object attached to a rope or chain and used to moor a vessel to the sea bottom," is used both symbolically and practically when it comes to stress management.

When we experience the wave of a big emotion, we can follow a path that can help us to regulate and stay open, rather than blow and/or disconnect. This path looks like this:

→ **Awareness of body**
With practice, we begin reconnecting with physical cues that our stress "temperature" is rising. For many, it's a tightened jaw, rigid and fast movements, or literally overheating. We can bring compassionate mindfulness to our bodies during times of rising stress.

→ **Name what is happening in your body**
Once we become mindful, we can practice saying aloud or in our head what is happening. This powerful parenting tool is called sportscasting: Naming what we observe within ourselves. This sounds like: "My body is becoming very rigid right now; I need support to destress."

→ **Connect to your sensory calming tool**
Finding a tool that soothes an overstimulated, or under-stimulated nervous system is a hero's journey! Through trial and error, as well as a commitment to exploration, we can find what works best for us. For some, it's deep and long exhales. For others, stepping outside and putting your feet onto the earth. For some, it's chewing gum. For others, it's grabbing a stress ball and squeezing it as hard as possible!

→ **Honor the process**
When we can move away from the urgency of "must be fixed now!" we can adopt a more loving and realistic mindset. We can meet ourselves where we are and trust that we will get through it. For some parents, saying aloud or in their heads, "we will get through this" or "this is temporary," supports them to connect to the process and patience and return to their green zone.

→ **Open to connection**
Here, we can begin to unlearn that experiencing stress equals disconnection. We can experience stress and also remain open to communication. This can be through communication, "Hey honey, I need support within myself right now, and I'm here for us." It can be somatic, like taking deep breaths and opening up your arms for your child to sit on your lap and breathe with you. It can be mental, and a voice in your head narrating, "It's safe. Turn back to your child. You can do this".

→ **Recommit to your child and present moment**
Once our stress cycle unwinds, you can recommit to your child, the moment, and forward movement. This may mean tending to your child's dysregulation and need for physical and emotional support. This may mean verbal problem-solving. This may be a silent commitment in your heart to lean in and show up.

BUILDING BRIDGES WITH EMPOWERED COMMUNICATION TOOLS

Once we commit to tracking our stress thermometer and engaging in our ANCHOR process, we can begin building new habits. Because yelling is a vocal expression of our flight or fight state within the nervous system, what would happen if we supported ourselves to shift away from nonproductive vocal strategies into productive ones?

Marshall Rosenberg, the founder and advocate of Nonviolent Communication, one of the core pillars of our methodology here at the Jai Institute for Parenting, says: "Yelling is the tragic expression of an unmet need." In plain English? Like children, our most and least desired behaviors as parents indicate a deeply complex inner world.

Take our earlier example of the dad who lost his temper at the dinner table. This parent was already running low on inner resources in the morning as he hadn't slept through the night and had just woken up! He probably began the day feeling slightly annoyed that he didn't sleep well. However, he did not stop, check in, drop his anchor, and name his experience. He didn't access the opportunity to communicate within himself about his state, needs, or feelings. (This can happen in 5 seconds! It does not need to be a laborious process).

The situation escalated into frustration and irritation with a wailing toddler on the ground. Dad longed for ease. He then experienced a racing heart and anxiety. He quickly could not tolerate the uncomfortable mixture of feelings of displeasure and unfulfilled longings.

In many homes, a parent would try and communicate his feelings and needs in a way like this:

"You need to start listening to me right now! You are not focusing and listening, and you are making me SO ANGRY! If you just listened to me the first time, I would not have to YELL!"

As we discover that we don't need to get to the point of losing it to meet our needs, we can then slowly evolve into Nonviolent Communication. We get to practice a foundational four-stage process:

1. Observation
2. Identifying feelings
3. Identifying needs
4. Making a developmentally appropriate, clear request

It could sound like this:

In a soft tone, with an open face, "Hey, sis, I see you're standing and staring at the t.v. instead of getting your shoes on. I'm beginning to feel nervous, and I'm hoping we can all focus. Are you willing to get your eagle eyes on and find your shoes? Do you need support, or are you willing to do it yourself?

Little brother, I hear you say that you are a dinosaur! I wonder, hmm, could you stomp like a dinosaur into your big boy shoes? Alright, team, let's blast off to the car!"

This may sound like something said only in rainbow-fairy-unicorn-land, but I can assure you that THIS is possible with practice. We can consciously own our overstimulated energy and funnel it down a productive path. Practicing this process out of the heat of the moment and when things are going well is useful. This way, this tool will not feel so foreign when we are under stress.

ALLOWING OUR CHILDREN THEIR ANGER

Chris's son was so angry. He was angry that he had a sister with autism. He was angry he had to go to school. He was angry at everything. Chris was mad that he was mad. She'd tell herself he had no right to be angry about having a special-needs sister. She wanted him to be different. The anger and resentment spiraled.

Two years ago, she separated from a destructive relationship with her husband. And then came the biggest blow: her son, who was a junior in high school, was no longer going to school and then lying about it, choosing instead to stay home and smoke pot all day in his room—her bright, deep, and beautiful son—moved in with his dad. He moved into an apartment below his father's house. Chris was deeply afraid of where he was headed. She also knew his father—who had been virtually absent as a parent—would not be providing any kind of guidance. She was so afraid of losing her son to his self-destruction and losing her connection to him because she rarely saw him.

Chris shares that this was the scariest time of her life:

> I would call him, and he wouldn't return my calls. His dad was the gatekeeper, and there was absolutely nothing I could do about it. Henry was avoiding me because I was actively trying to get him to stop smoking pot and nicotine. I helped him transfer to an independent study school as a way to help him reduce his anxiety, which had become part of a vicious cycle of missing school and getting behind on his work. He did not attend that school either, which only fed into his anxiety and the cycle of drug abuse. With his dad, he could simply do whatever he wanted, and I was going crazy worrying and calling him and getting absolutely nowhere—with Henry or with his dad.

> And that was when I let go. I accepted what was. I accepted that I no longer influenced Henry and his dad. I accepted that Henry was no longer a high school student. And I decided to just be there. I knew I had built a strong foundation. I'd worked hard for that. And I trusted that Henry knew it too.

> Slowly Henry came back to me. I eventually encouraged him to get a GED, which he completed in December of what would have been his senior year. When he had a mental health crisis a few months later, I was the person he called. He calls me for relationship advice. And work advice. And just to chat. And to tell me he loves me. That I'll "always be number one."

Recently, Henry shared that when the time comes that I will no longer be able to care for his sister, he will have a place for her to live with him. His autistic sister will forever need help. The sister who used to attack him in front of his friends, who required so much of my time and energy that he was often angry as a young boy. He has a big enough heart at age nineteen to forgive her, forgive me, and promise to take care of her when the time comes."

✳

So many kids are so freaking angry right now. And they have every reason to be. However, disavowing them of this anger or judging them for it is a path to disconnection and ultimately harm. To give our children's anger space and air, we must first learn to name and acknowledge our own. From this space of understanding, we provide a safe harbor for the expression of anger from our children.

Here's a powerful practice for allowing anger in others (whether the anger is coming from a child or an adult). First of all, let's just name anger for what it is: It's a feeling that sometimes causes people to act in less-than-pleasant ways. Most of the time, another person's anger won't hurt you. It may cause discomfort, but we are adults. We can handle discomfort, especially in service to the people we love!

Of course, it goes without saying that if physical safety is a risk, please, for the love of all things, get help and safety. Some kids will act out with physical aggression. Some adults will act out with physical aggression. If this is the case, you simply must get outside support, as defined in the introduction of this book.

However, if we're talking about a big expression of anger that won't actually hurt our bodies or any bodies, then we can use this visualization tool.

Imagine you are a reed planted in the dirt at the edge of a pond. Your roots run deep into the earth, webbed out deep and wide. A storm brews. The wind starts to blow. The water splashes up on the shore. The reed blows in the wind but remains rooted. It gets doused with water and bends the other way but remains rooted.

When confronted with an unhealthy expression of anger, an emotionally grounded person's role is just like the reed. We can allow ourselves to move with the wind but stay rooted to the earth. We don't need to defend against what can't hurt us. It's just like air. Hot air, perhaps, but we are movable, not breakable. We don't need to exert force back. Because just like the storm, when expressed, anger will dissipate.

Unfortunately, unhealthy expressions of anger are the norm. So it's not useful to expect other people to have healthy access to their anger, as much as we wish they did. It's far more useful to become a person who can tolerate all of the anger in the world, allowing it to wash over without adding more fuel to the proverbial fire.

I say this with the utmost compassion, having been on the righteous end of a relationship with someone who was often angry. Making someone else wrong for their anger doesn't help. Making our children wrong for their anger perpetuates the cycle that keeps so many people angry.

Being the safe space for another person to express their anger, so long as it is not harmful, is a powerful role. Because here's the magical thing: When we allow another person grace in the presence of their emotional outbursts, instead of fighting it, making it wrong, or shaming them, a powerful path to healing emerges.

When we allow a person to yell, or (in my son's case, hit the tree with a stick as hard as he could for as long as he wanted), or scream into a pillow or rage against indignity, the anger gets out. It's not pent-up.

Yelling loses its power when we don't yell back. Anger can be expressed differently when we don't get angry with anger. It can feel magical, but it's just psychology.

THE POSSIBILITY OF RUPTURE AND REPAIR

As we slowly mend the parts within ourselves that lean on unhealthy expressions of anger to move through stress and communicate our needs, we will inevitably fall; you may fall often and hard. For some, especially those disconnected from their body's sensations and feelings, it can take years to experience a consistent streak of self-regulation and emotional maturity. New communication patterns can take as much practice as learning a new language. Cultivating the awareness that gets in front of and prevents outbursts will take time to track and implement.

So, while you may feel desperate to shift your behaviors and shift them quickly, the stakes can feel unbearably high. Believing in the possibility of repair means we can be less afraid of making mistakes. Many parents who grew up in a home with yelling did not ever hear their parents take accountability, model self-empathy, or apologize for their mistakes. But we can break this cycle.

We are now learning that a rupture within the relationship does not mean the end. We can move through our remorse, grief, and even shame because we now have a light at the end of the tunnel: the possibility of repair.

Dr. Daniel Siegel, one of our heroes in our work here, shares that "you repair any breach in the relationship as quickly as possible." You want to restore a collaborative, nurturing connection with your child as soon as everyone has calmed down. Ruptures without repair leave both parent and child feeling disconnected. You can verbalize your regret and own your mistakes. You have an opportunity to model your humanity to your child and normalize that growth takes time and mistakes happen.

We will talk more deeply about conflict and repair in the next chapter.

THE MAGIC OF ANGER

Our anger is important. It lets us know when a boundary has been broken or a value has gone unmet. This data gives us feedback about what is happening in our external world. Anger is mobilizing. It spurs us to action. Heck, many of us became parenting coaches because we were really angry about how we were parented in our past and how we see children being parented in the present. Our anger catalyzes movements. It simply needs to be directed appropriately and effectively.

It is more than fine to be angry with our children when they break a rule or disregard family values and agreements. Communication is the pathway to sharing our anger without causing physical or emotional harm.

Letting our children see our anger and hear about our experience of anger paves the way for them to have an evolved understanding and relationship with anger themselves.

Try saying, "I'm feeling so angry right now. I feel my face getting hot, and my chest feels so tight. I'm going to go let my anger out, and then we can come back and talk about what happened."

Your anger is valuable. Communicate it while also taking responsibility for it.

When your child is angry, let it be ok! Try saying, "I can see you are really angry right now. I get it. How would you like to let your anger out?"

Some ideas for adults to access anger in healthy ways:

- Name it. Don't hold it in. Tell someone (or yourself) that you are angry.
- Dance your face off to your favorite rage song
- Squeeze or scream into a pillow as hard as you can.
- Go outside and scream your head off (Yes, I do sometimes let out a guttural yowl while driving alone in my car!)
- Journal: I am so angry that . . .
- Cry
- Shake your body (Notice that animals do this after an intense experience. This is wired nervous system regulation)

Have a good person in your life who can catch all of your true, intense feelings as they spill out (We like to call this a vomit bucket holder)

Some additional ideas to access your anger in healthy ways for children:

- Hit a tree trunk with a stick
- Color an angry drawing
- Write it down (if age appropriate)
- Be their vomit bucket holder
- Squeeze their whole body super tight and then shake like a tree in the wind

Finally, it is normal and healthy for children to want to play aggressively. Finding outlets for children to move this energy is important. Kids require movement—so find that jiu-jitsu class, let them climb the rocks, and play rough and tumble with friends. Yes, it will go too far sometimes. And you'll step in. But we must get over the idea that children are supposed to sit still like perfect little angels. That's so 1880!

A note on cultural experience:

Cultures and communities normalize anger and the expression of anger differently. Each family also creates norms and defines what is acceptable to them, alongside cultural context. In Ashley's Indian family, hitting babies on the wrist is considered acceptable as a useful tool for behavior correction. Richard is a black man who witnessed his father beat his mother with a shovel and was taught early that physical violence was just a part of life. Lina is of Chinese/Singaporean descent and shares that anger was not allowed to be expressed in her family ever, while simultaneously being encouraged to discipline children physically "but with a ruler, so they don't know it's you," she incredulously shares.

Understanding our personal values is so important. We are wired to stay connected to our community and maintain the status quo. Our values anchor us to our decisions about how we choose to live our lives and parent our children, especially if we are departing from our cultural norms and expectations.

We've heard over the years that there is fear, particularly in black communities, that disarming children from their anger and cultivating a nonviolent expression will make them less safe. Richard bravely shares that he simply decided that nonviolence was an immovable value for himself that was vital to instill in his children. He empowers his daughters to use their voices to stand up for themselves.

You get to decide what you will and won't tolerate, as expressions of anger, for yourself and your family. This is important, albeit messy, territory. Together I believe that we will find a more peaceful future as we cultivate this work, one brave family "doing it differently" at a time.

MAGNOLIA, AGE 7

What do you like most about the way your parents treat you?

When you sing to me when I'm about to go to bed.

How do we treat you?

I think you treat me goodly. And you treat me loveable and stuff.

Have you ever been punished for doing something wrong?

Yes.

Yes? Do you know what a punishment is?

Ummm. Yeah… Oh it means… No. What is it?

Well, like if you did something wrong and we made you go sit by yourself, or we took something away that you liked?

It would make me feel kinda mad at you guys and sad that you did that to me.

How do you know what the rules are?

I know what the rules are because you tell me them over and over again!

What are the rules?

The rules are don't jump on the couch and don't eat candy all of the time.

How do we treat each other in our family? With?

KINDNESS!!

Yes. That IS how we treat each other in this family. That's what Mommy and Daddy say all of the time, right?

Yes. But you also say no jumping on the couch and no eating candy all of the time.

What happens if you don't follow the rules?

You say, "Magnolia Sue, you may not do that!!!"

CHAPTER TEN

Radical Repair and Constructive Conflict

My stepmother abused my brother. As a kid, I remember thinking that I was getting off easy. She wasn't kind to me. But she didn't lock me in the bathroom or put tabasco in my mouth. When I was around twelve, she told me that women like us were lucky because if there were a nuclear war, our body fat would keep us alive longer than skinny women. She told me I was going to go to hell (because I wasn't Christened). She regularly tore apart my mother (even though they had been friends in their twenties).

She was manipulative and charming. She would pull me in close with her attention and then cruelly deliver a blow to my psyche with impressive force and guile.

The rage I felt because of what happened to us rose to the surface in therapy. Its target? My father. How did he stand by and allow all of this to happen?

I hadn't spoken to him in years, but after I'd written a Facebook post about some of the abuse we faced as kids, he messaged me: "Now I know why you hate me so much."

Ever the peacemaker, I answered: "I don't hate you, Dad. I hate what happened to us." He offered to get on a call, which we did a few days later. I broke down in sobs, speaking truths that had been bottled up inside of me for decades. I shared the hurts, the outcomes, and the consequences of his inaction with him.

And you know what he did? He defended every move. Played the victim. He told me, "I tried therapy, but I read the DSM-IV (this is the manual psychologists and psychiatrists use for mental health diagnoses) before I went, and so I figured out what was wrong with me and didn't think it would really help me."

He told me about their money struggles, fights, and toxic relationship. What he didn't say? That he understood my rage. That he could see how hard it must have been for his children. There was no acknowledgment that he bore any responsibility for what happened.

I've forgiven my father. And, he is not in our lives. I've surrendered the hope that there can be a different future than in the past.

I am desperate for other families to avoid the disconnection and separation resulting from an unacknowledged past.

There is nothing more humbling than Peaceful Parenting because it requires vulnerability. It happens in the depths of our human experience. Today's children won't stay in relationships with their parents out of obligation. They will stay in a relationship with their parents when it is *real*. Our culture has changed. Children are no longer bound by the ideas of duty and obligation that kept them connected to parents who treated them poorly. Rather than fear the potential of a future where our children no longer want to be in relationship with us, we can embrace the opportunity to develop a deep and unwavering bond.

Children who are respected, honored, and nurtured by their parents want to stay in a relationship with them.

As children, we interpret life through a very limited lens of understanding. When parents act poorly, there are two paths of interpretation:

- My parent wants to hurt me.
- I deserve to be hurt.

The brain is wired to assume the latter. A child relies on their parent for survival. Preserving connection with a parent (or any adult caregiver) is hard-wired into the most primitive aspects of the human brain.

So, when an adult child figures out that they weren't responsible for the harm they experienced as a child, there is often a confrontation with their parents, or as we hear more and more, distance, separation, and even cutting parents off completely. It happens all of the time. Not because the kids are ungrateful. Because they are furious.

Now, lest you think that this chapter is about never, ever, never making mistakes with our kids so that they don't leave you, allow me to disavow this as the point from the get-go. It's not about not making mistakes. It's about owning them.

Because of my experience with my father, in contrast with the mistakes I've made as a parent, I admire parents who authentically apologize when they act out of accordance with values and agreements.

Traditional parenting is based on a fundamental destructive belief: *The parent is always right.* If the parent admits they are wrong, the fear is they will lose control or their status or authority. And so what the parent says goes, regardless of the situation's fairness, logic, or truth.

"Because I said so."

"I'm an adult. You're a kid. I know better."

"Because I'm up here, and you're down there."

"This isn't a democracy."

This puts our kids in a double bind because being in a relationship with someone who always needs to be right, won't say they are sorry, and demands that they win every argument is brutal. When that person is your parent, you also deeply desire to be IN the relationship, even if it hurts.

Let's look at the ramifications of this dynamic clearly and honestly. We are teaching children that love looks like control. We are teaching them that love equals suffering. This perfectly sets people up for toxic and abusive relationships in the future because these patterns feel comfortable. They are known. They feel like love.

When real, unconditional love shows up, adults who were treated poorly by their parents don't know what to do with it. Codependency, control, and manipulation are way comfier.

Oof. Right?

Of course, I did everything not to marry a version of my father. But, many years later, I realized I exactly married my father. So many coaches we shared time with to write this book tell the same story. They married the person that made them feel safe because it felt *familiar*. And safety looked a lot like the dysfunction they experienced as kids. Some of the relationships made it, and some didn't.

The primary relationship between the caregiver and child sets the stage for every future relationship that a child will have. No pressure or anything.

As adults, we must tend to our defensiveness. Our defensiveness is human. It is the desire to protect ourselves from feeling pain. When we look underneath the surface of defensiveness, we usually find shame. Shame is a very uncomfortable feeling. So we learned, early on, that we should armor ourselves instead of feeling it. Defensiveness comes from the inner voice that tells us that if we've done something bad, we ARE bad. That a transgression of any kind defines us. So many people who grew up with angry parents cannot cope with their mistakes because of the self-judgment and self-hatred they learned from their parents.

I've come to believe this is the root of what happened with my dad. He simply couldn't take responsibility because it would have been too damaging to his ego. Sad, yes. But also so, so common.

Here are some sneaky ways defensiveness shows up:

Gaslighting: Making our reaction another person's fault.

Bypassing: Hearing and knowing a person's experience and negating it, invalidating it, or assuming it's no big deal.

Attacking: Using our words or physical body to hurt another person.

Avoidance: Removing ourselves from communication and connection.

Righteousness: Needing to be right when presented with conflict.

Fabrication: Lying to absolve ourselves of personal responsibility.

Denial: Claiming to be unaware of the circumstances and their impact.

Victimhood: Claiming something happened to make a person act in a harmful way.

Becoming defensive doesn't mean you're a bad person. It just means you're a human person. All of us have defensive tendencies. The opportunity here is to become aware of our defensiveness so that it doesn't create walls between the people we love the most and us. You see, defensiveness does an excellent job of keeping us from feeling the pain of shame. But it also does an excellent job of building walls between our kids (and the other people in our life) and us.

Defensiveness leaves no space for resolution. Over time, resentment builds. We can all identify someone in our life who wasn't willing to meet us in the messy middle. Leaving things unsaid means they'll be carried within us, whittling away at our sense of self. Not allowing our children the space to say what needs to be said means that they will carry this burden, too.

If you aren't yet intimately familiar with your defensiveness, you're not alone. We all have very sneaky ways of avoiding conflict and shame. Just recently, my life partner was upset with me. I was late, again. I tend to underestimate the time it will take me to do too many things (Hi. ADHD brain here. Nice to meet you.) Because of this, I've developed a very laissez-faire relationship with time. Outside of work, it doesn't bother me when people are late. But it bothers him. When he's frustrated, I play one of two cards: The flake or the victim. I am not a flake nor a victim, but I've been effectively (well, maybe that's up for debate!) using these defenses since I was a kid!

"OH! Was that paper due today? Silly me, you don't mind if I get it to you tomorrow, do you?" Smile. (Flake card. Check.)

"You don't know how hard I work and how much I do for everyone else! Don't I get some leeway with time?" (Victim card. Check.)

"I'm SO sorry, officer! I didn't realize that I was driving so fast. The book I am listening to is just SO GOOD."

The path to softening our defensiveness is simple, but it's not easy. It's to allow other people to share the impact that we've had on them and really, actually hear them. When I stopped making excuses for why I was late and allowed myself to empathize with the stress, inconvenience, and frustration my partner was feeling, I could hear something different than "you're a bad person for being late." (Something I've been hearing my whole life).

I could hear, "this is important to me, and I'm wondering if you can just communicate with me when your plans change," which was an easy yes.

OWN YOUR AWFUL

All of us have darker aspects of our personality and psyche. We all have rage. We all have fear. We all have insecurity, frustration, and even the potential to enact violence. Society, culture, and family tell us to ignore and judge ourselves for these tendencies. But until we acknowledge and come into a relationship with the darker aspects of ourselves, we can't support our kids to do the same.

It's the rare person who makes it to mid-life without some serious integrity breaches or who hasn't acted in a way that elicits shame. Our past failures, mistakes, and wrongs can either define us or teach us. They can be the reason we keep telling ourselves that we don't deserve all of the beautiful things, or they can be the fodder for our growth and evolution.

When we choose the latter and give our children visibility into our own process for coming to terms with the choices and actions we aren't proud of, we give them an extraordinary gift. They discover that it's o.k.

to make mistakes and that they are worthy of love, regardless of bad decisions or bad grades. They see that growth is a lifelong process.

When Jenny's son was six, his behavior started to change drastically. This sweet, kind, and gentle boy began to exhibit rage. He'd always been super snuggly and close with Jenny. But out of nowhere, he began to threaten her physically. After baseball practice, he chased her around the house with his bat, threatening to hit her. It wasn't playing. He was incredibly serious. After a game of Chutes and Ladders, Jenny's son became very upset because she won the game. He drew a picture of a knife with blood dripping off of it and stabbing his mom. He showed her the picture, and Jenny, of course, burst into tears.

She said, "O.k., you're upset. I get it. Let's take a break, honey. I'm going to go to my quiet space, and you can go to yours. It's going to be o.k." She made it to her bathroom, where she collapsed on the floor in a pool of tears. Several minutes later, there was a knock on the door. It was her child, also in tears.

"Mommy, Mommy . . . I didn't mean it. I love you, Mommy." They sat on the floor of the bathroom and just held each other for a very long time. Eventually, he shared, "I don't know what's happening. I just feel like I have to do these mean things."

Jenny shares that she doesn't think they'd ever held each other so tightly. She assured him that he was o.k. That she loved him too. And that they would figure it out together.

After several doctor's visits, the culprit was identified: Bartonella, a tick-borne disease that can cause rage.

Imagine a different outcome where Jenny told him he was bad, broken, or evil, or where he was shamed, blamed, or punished. His illness would have continued undetected.

When we don't initiate repair with children after highly charged or traumatic experiences, they will internalize the experience through self-labeling. Or, they'll do everything they can to reject the label and become rebellious. They will turn things around and create a narrative that destroys self-worth and self-confidence.

I believe our children deserve our willingness to lay down our defenses and ego. In our humility, vulnerability, and willingness to hear, see, and witness their experience, even when it hurts so much, or if we don't get it, or are telling ourselves they shouldn't feel the way they feel, we are paving the way for a very different future for our child.

Because then, they won't expect love to hurt. They will expect love to accept. They will expect love to be forgiving and gracious.

This flies in the face of the idea that we need to toughen up our kids because the "real world won't coddle them." This idea is damaging parent/child relationships every single day. We teach our kids how to allow others to treat them. When they are unconditionally loved and cared for by their parents, they are armed with self-confidence and self-worth instead of defense mechanisms. They will be far better equipped to navigate challenging people and circumstances. Period.

Inevitably, we are going to have times when we mistreat our kids. We are going to lose our temper and yell. We will project our stress, frustration, or fear onto them. Sometimes we aren't going to be the parent we want to be. Please read this twice: IT. IS. O.K.

IT IS O.K.!

You are a person, imperfect, messy, and all. So are your kids. So when they see you mess up and then clean up your mess, they are being shown that they can make mistakes, too. Through modeling responsibility, they learn that it is their responsibility to clean up their messes, too.

The most secure, trust-based, long-lasting relationships experience challenges, learn from them, and grow because of them. Shared adversity creates a solid bond and a history of overcoming obstacles. Relationships like this have depth. They can withstand tragedies and losses.

As you develop the skills (and self-trust) to clean up your messes, you will notice something extraordinary happening with those you invite along with you. The love you already have for them will expand exponentially. And the love they have for you will do the same. When we speak of advocating for our children, this process is one of the most powerful tools we bring to bear. We are advocating for them by taking responsibility for what is ours, without shame, blame, or guilt, and paving a new path forward in our relationship.

THE CLEANUP JOB

The path to repair starts within ourselves through self-empathy. Acknowledging our mistakes to ourselves and allowing the process of sitting in the discomfort of their consequences is the first antidote to defensiveness.

Self-empathy is the willingness to accept, without judgment, how you feel. It's the willingness to name your feelings and take the initiative to get your own needs met. Self-empathy is a pause button for our reactivity and defensiveness.

When you can access authentic self-apology and forgiveness, you will anchor yourself in internal safety. Only then will your apology to your child land in a way that balances their inner disequilibrium and supports and repairs your relationship. After a mistake, as soon as you can, engage in this self-apology process. You can do it in your head or write it down. There are benefits to both processes.

SELF-APOLOGY FOR INNER SAFETY

- Name what happened.
- Name how you feel about what happened.
- Name what you felt before you reacted.
- Name what need was not being met for you.
- Name how your mistake impacted your child (feelings and needs).
- Make a commitment for next time.

Example: *Tonight, I screamed at my child to get in bed instead of supporting them gently. I had aggressive body language. I feel disappointed and heartbroken about what happened. Before I screamed, I felt desperate and exhausted. I needed support and rest. My child became very frightened and started to cry, making bedtime even longer. I dishonored their need for respect, gentleness, and safety. Next time, I will notice my body's stress cues, engage my ANCHOR, and stop before I scream. Even though I'm sad, I deserve forgiveness. I forgive myself for being human and missing an opportunity to be gentle and kind.*

Forgive. Let yourself know that you deserve forgiveness, and ruptures are an opportunity to reconnect and deepen your relationship with your child.

Once you've found safety within yourself, you can begin the process of creating repair with your child.

RECIPE FOR A MEANINGFUL REPAIR

We don't initiate repair because we need or expect something from our children. We initiate repair to take responsibility for our actions and come back into connection and trust. We make commitments on how we will act differently in the future, should the circumstance arise again.

Here's the process:

1. Connect
2. Ask consent
3. I imagine that you're feeling _____
4. Because of my choice to _____
5. I regret how I _____, because it caused you to_____
6. In the future, I'll do my best to _____
7. Here's what I'll do right now (my calming strategies) _____
8. For now, would it support you if _____

Example:

"Hi sweetie, is it okay if I come into your room? Whatcha working on? I was hoping to apologize for what happened earlier today; are you open to that?

Ok, thank you. I imagine you are feeling a bit confused about what happened this morning because of how I became very stressed and screamed at you. I regret how I lost control because it caused you harm. You became very stressed too and shut down. We were hoping for a smooth morning, but it became very tense.

Next time, I'm going to get everything ready BEFORE the morning. That way, I'm not rushing. That will help me stay calm. For now, would it be okay if I gave you a big hug? I love you, and I will keep trying to be your safe place."

Notice that we are not asking for forgiveness. The child gets to take their time. There is no urgency to fix the mistake. The child regaining safety through our modeling of self-accountability is the goal.

There's a reason we don't ask for forgiveness: It's often empty. The idea that we can take responsibility with a simple "I'm sorry" can be a defense mechanism all on its own. *"We'll just sweep that awfulness under the rug and act like it's not there!"*

Sorry, but saying sorry isn't enough. Not when we hurt someone we love. And not when someone we love hurts us. Connection, communication, and agreements are the empowered path forward.

We create fertile soil for real forgiveness through empathy. We can allow ourselves to receive the experience, thoughts, and feelings of the other person, even if we don't understand them or agree with them. When we can feel what the other person felt and acknowledge the role we played in the situation, quieting our inner voice that wants to say "but . . . But . . . BUT!" we gain trust. Mutual trust between parents and children is the goal.

A NOTE FOR PARENTS OF OLDER CHILDREN

Forgiveness doesn't have a timetable. If your child has years of evidence (whether deserved or not) that you haven't been a safe person for them, this process can take some time. If a late-teen or adult child comes to you and wants to share the impact of your parenting through their worldview, resist the urge to explain, defend, or deny their experience. Simply listen.

Chris shares:

> I occasionally call my son to apologize when I realize
> a mistake I made years earlier. It's not too late for me

to acknowledge it, and regardless of his response, I'm always glad when I do.

When my son was seventeen, my husband and I separated, and my best pal and favorite boy moved in with his father. I expected us to have 50/50 custody, but when your kid is seventeen, he can do what he wants, and what he wanted was to have an apartment at his dad's house, where he had little supervision. I was devastated.

One day, my estranged husband was out of town, and I couldn't reach my son. I drove over to his house to discover that, despite our repeated conversations, he was hosting a party. Pot and tequila were everywhere. I was infuriated. I sent everybody home. I threatened to call the police. I insisted on searching his apartment and then insisted he come to my house for the night. Who knows what else I said? I was out of my mind.

Recently, as I was doing this Peaceful Parenting work, it hit me: I was parenting out of fear. I was SO afraid that this new arrangement meant I would lose my son. I wouldn't get to be his mom anymore. It wasn't the party itself. It was what it represented to me.

I picked up the phone and told him about my epiphany. "I was parenting out of fear," I said.

"Well, that's not a great way to do it," he replied. "And it's o.k., Mom," he said. Even if he hadn't said that and left it with a "Yeah, that was awful," it would have been o.k. with me. I did my part in making the repair.

If you would like to initiate this conversation, the most powerful statement to deploy is, "I've realized that I haven't always been a safe person for you. I would love to hear about some of your experiences as a child from your perspective.

You may be met with silence, stonewalling, or denial. Remember, defensiveness is a hard-wired human tendency. Let their response be o.k. Resist the urge to fill the silence. If they are unwilling to go there with you now, it's o.k. Try again. It may take a while for your child to believe you mean it. Even when they open up, they may take some time to trust that you can hear them without re-arming yourself with your defensiveness. Understand that this is perfectly normal. If it takes a month, year, or decade, this is your child. Keep showing up. It's never too late, and there is almost always a path back to reconnection. Please reach out for support from a parenting coach or mental health professional if you need guidance.

CONSTRUCTIVE CONFLICT

Growth doesn't happen when we're happy, satisfied, and content. Growth happens when we are uncomfortable. If we weren't uncomfortable, we wouldn't need to change. We have an ego that will deploy every trick available to our psyche to keep us from changing the status quo, so familiarity is the lounge-chair-by-the-pool-with-a-mojito for the ego.

In relationships, conflict is uncomfortable. So it is where we grow.

Listen, I think I am the most conflict-avoidant, people-pleasing, please-God-let-everyone -be-happy person on the planet (*and I know I'm in excellent company*). I hate conflict. But I'm learning to be good at it. Because avoiding it has hurt so many people I love, including myself.

Without space for conflict, there isn't space for buy-in or accountability. We unconsciously resort to the power dynamics that we are here to obliterate. So, uncomfortable as it is, we get to cozy up to conflict.

Conflict arises when two or more people have competing needs/wants, or desires. The conflict is not the problem. The problem is that the conflict often escalates to personal attacks, hurt feelings, and airing out past, unresolved grievances. Unhealthy conflict is why we've all learned to do everything we can to avoid it. But healthy conflict is the path to cooperation and compromise.

Conflicts are going to happen. They are going to happen with our kids, between our kids, between our co-parents and kids, and between our co-parents and us. So maybe let's get a bit comfier being uncomfy while becoming skilled at healthy conflict in relationships.

The discomfort you may feel during a conflict can't actually hurt you. It's just discomfort, so practice feeling it! A great way to practice is probably happening all of the time (if you have more than one child): sibling bickering, one of the most common complaints we hear when we survey parents about their biggest challenges. So practice being with your discomfort by (gasp!) letting them bicker. They've got an interpersonal challenge, so give them space to navigate it, noticing what's happening to your nervous system. Work on staying calm, even in the chaos of their fight.

This does two things: It gives your kids space to resolve their challenges on their own and develop healthy conflict resolution skills, AND it teaches you a lot about staying grounded while uncomfortable.

Some key skills of Constructive Conflict:

1. Surrender the need to be right or to win.
2. State your case clearly and directly.
3. Stay open and willing to hear the other party's perspective.

4. Resist dredging up past conflicts.
5. Don't make it personal. Don't take it personally.
6. Remain flexible. Be willing to offer concessions and make compromises.
7. Be kind to yourself and others. Constructive conflict takes practice!
8. When consensus is reached, agree and let it go!!
9. Embrace this powerful concept: "There's no right solution. There are lots of right options!"

As a coach, I can't tell you how many times I've heard people get what they want in conflict and continue fighting. This is because our nervous system has taken over the operations of the reasoning centers of the brain. If you're getting too escalated, take a break: *"Can we take fifteen minutes so I can tend to myself? We can pick this back up then."*

Having a culture of constructive conflict in your family is empowering. I can only speak for myself, but I feel a deep inner sense of pride when I have a conflict with my kids, and they can advocate for themselves with inner authority. This is what we want, isn't it? It is gratifying to be the leader who can give our children the space to find their voice in conflict.

When we come to an agreement or consensus, we have explicit buy-in. Having explicit buy-in is vital for accountability. We hold each other accountable to our agreements through the Empowered Communication framework in Chapter Eight.

When the conflict is with your spouse or co-parent about your kids

As you've gathered by now, parenting is rife with complexities, entrenched beliefs, fears, and expectations. Our own challenges are challenging enough. Then we add a whole other human being's stuff to the equation. This can be a recipe for relationship disaster (writing this while saying "duh" to myself).

Allyn shared a story about a time that her husband, Chris, got furious at dinner. He yelled at the kids because he felt they were being disrespectful. He called them spoiled and bratty. Her daughter, Nina, burst into tears and ran to her room, crying, *"I don't even belong in this family."*

Of course, Chris and Allyn wish the situation had gone differently, but it happened. He wasn't in the space to create repair (he'd had a very stressful day at work). Allyn stepped in. She loves her husband and empathized with his outburst.

She tended to the repair: *"Nina, sometimes when Daddy is stressed and worried, he says things he doesn't mean. Can you think of how sometimes Mommy does that, too? How about you? Do you ever say things you don't mean when you're angry?"*

This was an act of grace. Empathy is our superpower as peaceful parents, for our little people and our big people. Of course, she later had a conversation with Chris. He recognized that he had a bad reaction and needed to have the ability to step away when he had a bad day at work. Modeling constructive conflict and radical repair does wonders for the people in our world… The people we love.

Our parenting coach Chris (not Allyn's husband), had to step in more assertively, as she had a more domineering ex-husband who was causing emotional harm to her children. She stepped into protective mode, as it was necessary for her family. Sadly, not everyone is capable of the radical personal responsibility required for Peaceful Parenting. For some, this can be marriage ending. But not always. Chris felt that it was important to put her children in an environment where they were treated with respect.

She would tell them, *"You don't deserve to be yelled at. You deserve love, care, kindness, and respect and to be spoken to with love, care, and kindness. I told them that nothing they had done or could ever do warranted the yelling. I also wanted them to know that having a bad day wasn't a valid excuse for treating somebody else poorly—it wasn't o.k. for their dad to do that to them, nor was it o.k. for them to take out their frustrations on somebody else."*

Lina was recently on a shopping excursion with her three-year-old, her baby, and her husband. Let's face it, Walmart can make the most regulated among us lose it when we've got our whole family in tow. She lost it and yelled at her son. On the way home, the situation escalated, and Lina got in a fight with her husband, a rip-roaring one, with the kids in the back seat. She asked him to let her out of the car so she could decompress. "I'll get an Uber," she said. This triggered his defensiveness, and he started yelling back. Pretty soon, everyone was crying.

Later that night, when the kids were asleep, the couple processed the fight together so they could understand what was happening beneath the anger and frustration shown earlier in the day. But because the fight happened in front of their kids, even though their son was only three, Lina felt she needed to create safety and repair with her child.

The next day, when the boy came home from school, Lina and her husband talked calmly with him about their inability to stay calm. They apologized to their child, acknowledged that they scared him, and promised to do better the next time. More importantly, the incident was not the child's fault. It was a simple short conversation that is age appropriate for the child's young development, and the family ended it with a little bit of storytelling and hugs. Between the couple, though, they made a renewed commitment to practice the tools they have learned before in therapy on how to embrace healthy conflict.

Here's my recommendation: If you are navigating this work for yourself, stay in your lane as much as possible. You being "right" or them making you "wrong" isn't going to make anything better for your kids. So do your best to practice and integrate these tools for yourself before trying to convince anyone else that your way is the only way.

"It's rarely good advice to give advice to those who haven't asked for it."

When we work with clients as parenting coaches, we never give advice without consent, and we coach our clients to ask for consent in giving advice to their kids before giving it. This is a bold new world of respect for children and adults alike.

Kids are so incredibly resilient. It takes one parent meeting their needs as a peaceful parent to absorb nearly all of the benefits. My own children's dad isn't a very introspective person. He's reactive and controlling (and also funny and charming!) They can separate his less-than-awesome moments from their own identity. He's taught them quite a bit about emotional competency and effective communication. So, do I wish he could be more kind? Of course. But he's been an important part of my children's growth. It doesn't look how I want it to look. But that's the deal. And my acceptance of who he is (and isn't) makes the whole situation far less volatile than it could be.

But what blows me away is that the kids have learned to stand up for themselves! They aren't intimidated by him. They are brave. And they aren't scared of conflict or confrontation. It isn't always comfortable, but it is what I want for them and the future that they will create for themselves.

MASON, AGE 13

What do you notice about what is different about the way you are parented than your friends?

There's a lot more trust and a lot more freedom. It's less strict, but we understand the rules. They don't need to be policed. If I'm having an issue I can talk to you about it. It's not a secret.

How does that affect your perspective of relationships?

It makes communication easier. I can express what I'm feeling. If someone upsets me, I can share my feelings and what I want to experience. I don't let peers treat me poorly, and I'm not someone who will go along to get along.

CHAPTER ELEVEN

The Joy of Parenting

"Joy is happiness that persists regardless of external circumstances."

I was sitting at my dining room table, having just finished eating the positively delicious breakfast my teenage son had made me for Mother's Day.

My son stood up, picked up my plate, and said to my daughter, "Let's do the dishes and clean up the kitchen. I'll wash, and you dry and put away."

We chatted as they took care of me. I loved them with all of my heart. And I have made so many mistakes. And fought with them. And cried. And lost my mind. And wanted to run away. And then loved them as much as is humanly possible.

It was a peaceful, beautiful moment of caring and cooperation.

When they were finished, my son hugged me goodbye. And then he hugged his sister—his autistic sister who for so many years had made him so angry and resentful that he refused to touch her at all—and he said, "I love you SO MUCH, Maddie."

And I realized that despite my many mistakes, I had taught my kids how to love. And be loved.

The newfound peace in my house was now met with newfound peace inside myself. Peace in knowing I had done enough—and BEEN enough—for my kids. ~Chris Irvine

✴

Parenting is the path to personal growth and transformation. Our children are our growth partners. When we become better people, they become better people.

We are going to make mistakes. And so are they. But when the foundation of mutual trust and respect is maintained and established, there's nothing we can't handle together.

Fulfillment is the destination of Peaceful Parenting. We fulfill our promise to give our children the guidance they need to become responsible adults. You'll catch glimpses of nirvana as a peaceful parent. Perhaps you'll see your children enraptured in conversation with each other or witness them simply being themselves as they play in the yard. You'll admire their choices. Sometimes. But when you disagree with them, you know you'll work it out, the relationship fully intact.

Grace is the path of Peaceful Parenting. It is the gift you can give yourself and your children.

And fun. Fun is vital. So let's play. Whether our children are two or twenty-two, there is always fun to be had.

WHY PLAY?

Play is, quite literally, a child's sacred work. It is their contribution to life, their developing sense of self, their language, their lens, and their lifeblood. But more importantly, play creates fertile soil for connection, shared positive experiences, family lore, and joyous rituals. Play is as important for parents as children.

Psychiatrist Stuart Brown, the author of *Play*, says: "Play is something done for its own sake," and "It's voluntary, it's pleasurable, it offers a sense of engagement, it takes you out of time. And the act itself is more important than the outcome."

BENEFITS OF PLAY

Physical: Active play helps children with coordination, balance, gross and fine motor skills, and cultivating a healthy relationship with their environment. Cross-lateral movement in play (crawling, climbing, reaching across the body to retrieve objects) stimulates a healthy connection between the left and right hemispheres of the brain.

Emotional: While playing and activating the social engagement system, children can experience strong emotions like anger, fear, shame, and sorrow, in a way that is digestible for them. Acting out these emotions and role-playing through them supports children to diffuse any pent-up painful memories of these emotions and create a secure attachment to them. This develops emotional regulation as they age. It's never too late to begin this practice.

Social: Play helps children develop an awareness of social cues, empathy, collaboration, and negotiation.

Cognitive: Play is every child's learning language. It ignites their social engagement system, which puts their brain at ease. When the brain is flooded with stress and pressure to learn, the brain is flooded with fear and will not retain what it's learning. Alternatively, it can begin to associate learning with stress and limiting beliefs like "I'm stupid" or "I'm not capable." The more joy and less pressure our children experience in their learning process, the better their brains develop. Play can also improve executive functioning skills like following directions, making a plan, remembering what the parent said to the child, and executing tasks with follow-through.

Creative: Imagination without any direction or interruption brings children to a place where "anything is possible." This nourishes their prefrontal cortex, the space in their brain where genius occurs. Imagination IS the pathway to genius, innovation, and infinite possibilities.

Communication: Play allows children to practice communication in a low stakes arena. They act out and practice the nonviolent communication you are modeling, and they diffuse any words of violence or other stress they have heard throughout their life.

THE SCIENCE OF PLAY

Play is surrendering to the present moment. It is the epitome of the nervous system state of social engagement. Play flows when we feel safe in our bodies. Play supports both a child and an adult to de-stress and return to safety from within. With nervous system science in mind, understanding that play is the social engagement that brings life, we recognize how exercising playfulness and actively playing with our children nurtures our children's sense of security and belonging to themselves, their families, and the life around them.

Play, especially unstructured play (outdoors whenever possible), provides an opportunity for our children to meet their inherent limitations, bypass the limitation of time and space, and develop their prefrontal cortex. Remember, this is the area of the brain where executive functioning happens, like conscious decision-making, understanding of long-term consequences for short-term decisions, and being willing to compromise or collaborate as a teammate toward a shared goal.

NAEYC (National Association for the Education of Young Children) has called play a "central component in developmentally appropriate practice," and the United Nations High Commission on Human Rights declared it a "fundamental right of every child." Play is not frivolous. It is not something to do after the 'real work' is done. It is not something to do. *Play is the real work of childhood.* Through it, children have their best chance for becoming whole, happy adults."

So what keeps us from being playful? For some parents, playing with their children is akin to pulling teeth without anesthesia. We KNOW it's good for our children, for us, and our relationship with our children, but we struggle, nonetheless.

For many parents, this is a source of great shame and avoidance due to:

Lack of safety in childhood: As a child, play may not have been prioritized in your everyday world. If you were raised in a home without emotional safety, or if you were raised by an adult who "couldn't" play, your ability to access play, awe, wonder, and imagination may have been blocked. We may believe that letting go and surrendering to presence is not safe, and we struggle with feeling out of control when our child is directing the play.

Lack of emotional connection in childhood: We were not met with vulnerable, emotional connection. Play requires presence, which is the most intimate and vulnerable expression of our humanity.

When we experience trauma, our systems can either process the overwhelming energetic charge or not. Whether or not your system was able to process that energy at the time of the trauma has NOTHING to do with your ability, capacity, or function. It has everything to do with the external circumstances that followed a traumatic event.

Our systems want to be able to process what happened, but they need the conditions necessary to do so. Those conditions include safety after the event ends and a mutually empathetic witness. This witness is someone who can hold space for our experience and remain anchored in safety for us while also dipping into the state we are in to attune with our experience and support us to feel less alone in it. They create the possibility for our systems to do what they have the natural intelligence and capacity to do: to gain freedom from what happened to us.

When we didn't experience these conditions, our system was left replaying the traumatic event, and our protective parts show up lovingly to do their best to be sure what happened never happens again.

Play is an experience of regulation and, in many ways, mimics what our systems (now, as adults) are saying was dangerous in the past. So we want to begin stepping toward play gently.

Consider the following:

Might you be able to explore play with a pet or a child?

Can you tolerate watching dogs play or kids playing at the park?

What about playing with creativity, having a game night, dancing alone, listening to a playful song, and taking it in?

Play is an act of incredible healing, and however you relate to it now makes so much sense. You can take one brave step at a time.

WHEN SHOULDN'T WE BE PLAYFUL?

It's important to be in tune with what children communicate nonverbally and verbally. If they're already dysregulated, adult-initiated play may feel unsafe and chaotic to them.

Similarly, if children are experiencing any sort of trauma, the uncertainty and novelty of play may be anything but grounding to them. In this instance, they need a solid and peaceful connection through co-regulation before their nervous systems will be open to anything resembling fun.

Likewise, if the adult feels anxious, angry, or escalated in any way, children can perceive their play as aggressive—and will therefore be unreceptive to it.

Play works best when both parent and child are emotionally grounded and in tune with one another. The second best is when the adult feels fully regulated and sees the child starting to dysregulate. Here, the adult may be able to bring the child back to a regulated state through gentle, slow, and intentional play.

DISCOVERING YOUR PLAY LANGUAGE

Each of us has a natural play language. To be playful is not just to be silly and active. It's about being connected to our natural expression of joyfulness. For some parents, playfulness means going rock climbing. For others, their idea of play is cuddling on the couch and reading books with their child. You get to be yourself in your play, and your children can be themselves!

We learn to embrace our natural language of play, filling ourselves with clarity, confidence, and security. This way, we can more easily enter our child's play language. The resentment won't be as strong, or won't exist, because you are grounded in what brings you joy and consciously choose to enter your child's expression of joy. The closer you are to your joy, the more willing and calm you will be in boundary-setting with your child around playtime. You will have more energy, enthusiasm, and more S P A C E to practice and be joyful.

PERMISSION TO THRIVE

So many people seem to want to connect in suffering. Complaining about kids, spouses, and neighbors becomes a social currency. You don't need to participate.

The culture of complaint keeps us stuck focusing on what isn't going well in our relationships. Sure, our brains will release the feel-good chemical dopamine when we engage in gossip or negative talk (we are wired to perceive this as connection), but the temporary high isn't worth the act's consequences.

You get to thrive as a parent. You get to LOVE parenting. You get to admire and adore your children. You get to enjoy family dinners and long car rides. Don't believe the ideas about how parenting is supposed to look. Decide for yourself what parenting will look like on your terms.

One humble, vulnerable and authentic step at a time. The connection between parent and child is formative for both parent and child. As we realize that we are growing ourselves up as we grow them up, we can be gentler and kinder along the way.

Choose your parenting moments, meaning the times when a more assertive, firm approach is necessary. When your kids are annoying, perhaps you can simply remove yourself from the room or put on some earbuds. When they are being unsafe, you can lean in.

The kids are going to be alright.

Let them be. I don't mean leave them alone. I mean BE. They have far more ability, wisdom, creativity, and intelligence than we give them credit. The more they have the opportunity to allow their natural gifts to shine, the more confident they will be in their natural gifts. Let. Them. Be.

So, dear parent, here's a last dose of inspiration for you. There is no better way to change the world than to change how you parent your child. Yes, they are the key to a better future for us all. But their ability to step into their destiny is wholly dependent on… YOU.

And so, truly, you hold the power to change the world. One peaceful moment at a time.

A 5-MINUTE DAILY PARENTING PRACTICE

At the end of each day, it's useful to journal:

What went well with my kids today:

What am I celebrating:

What does each child need from me tomorrow:

Then, I like to send a little love balloon from my heart to theirs. Simply beaming all the love, pride, adoration, and care I feel right into their hearts.

From the Mouths of Babes

My 15-year-old daughter and I recently visited my mom. Sitting at the kitchen counter having breakfast, my mom asked a question out of the blue:

"Can you help me understand? So, if Charlotte did something wrong, she would get in trouble, right? She'd be grounded or punished? Would you take her phone away?"

"What would be an example of something she might do wrong?" I asked.

"Well, say she got in a car with someone who was drinking."

Charlotte said, "Mom would just talk to me about it." "Yes," I continued. "I'd share how scared this made me. I'd ask that we create some new agreements so this wouldn't happen again."

"You realize, Nana, that if I got punished all the time, I wouldn't come to Mom the next time I got in trouble."

Of course, as a teenager, I was grounded often. I could see the awareness growing in my mom. I got in real trouble as a teen because I feared her reaction and its repercussions. I thought I had to figure it all out myself. Trust is the outcome of Peaceful Parenting. And trust is what saves lives.

I asked Charlotte if she would be willing to record a conversation with me about her perspective on parenting. This also inspired the conversations with the children of Jai Coaches you've read through this book.

You see? The kids are, indeed, more than alright. The kids, when given the gift of unconditional love and radical acceptance? They are amazing.

CHARLOTTE, AGE 15

So this is just a conversation about what you've noticed about how you've been parented versus maybe some of your friends, some of the gifts you've given you, but also maybe some of the challenges.

So the first question is, how are you aware that the way you've been parented is different from your peers?

Something I've noticed since I was in kindergarten when I'd go to my friends' houses was how their parents would talk to them and talk to me, for that matter. Sometimes, other people's parents would yell at me, and I'd think, why are you yelling at me? It was very confusing for me as a child. Growing up, I got used to it, but I could still see my friend's parents would be super short-tempered. They would yell at their kids. They wouldn't communicate with them. I could see that there wasn't healthy communication.

Even as a little kid, you could see that.

Yeah. I had a friend who wanted to put ketchup in mac and cheese. And her mom said, "NO! You can't put ketchup in mac and cheese." I thought to myself, just let her put ketchup in the mac and cheese. It's not that deep.

So as you think about these differences, how do you think that that's made a difference in the relationship you and I have versus some of the relationships you witnessed between your teenage friends and their parents?

Am I allowed to talk about dad's parenting?

Sure.

Because as a friend, I'm more likely to hear all the grievances people have with their parents. You don't see everything, and if it's a friend you haven't known for a long time, it's harder to speak to their relationship and past history with their parents.

As opposed to me comparing my two parents, where I know the full experience and can see how it's easier to be honest and be open about things with you. It's easier to come to you about things when I'm not afraid you'll be mean to me. I'm not going to get my phone taken away. I'm not going to get grounded. I'm not going to get screamed at. I'm not going to feel awful about it. And I can get help in situations where I need help instead of not saying anything because I'm afraid of the repercussions.

If you could put yourself into the shoes of someone whose parents aren't understanding in that way or trying to control their behavior. What do you think the flip side of that is? What do you think that does to their self-esteem or self-confidence?

After a certain amount of time, it makes it harder to bounce back to the good, you know, like you can only compartmentalize people so much, including your parents. And I think that after constantly facing punishments, you start to resent them.

When you resent people, it's really hard to enjoy time with them. It could basically not ruin, but corrupt the good moments. Because then, in the good moments, you could think, "oh, at what point is this gonna switch?" You probably have to filter yourself. Because you don't know what you can and can't say, because you could be getting yelled at, you could get punished. You might think they'll constantly bring up the past, so you don't get to be a different person.

Has anything been challenging for you because you've been parented differently?

Like I said before when I would go to friends' houses and my parents, friends would be awful to them or me. But even when you're really friends with someone, and they're being treated badly, if it's a parent who yells, you can't really say anything to them. It's not your place as their child's friend to say that's not right... You shouldn't be acting that way. Even though, in a lot of cases, they shouldn't.

So that was challenging for you because I'm hearing you felt a bit powerless in those situations.

Yeah.

How about with teachers who are more authoritarian?

One of the challenges is finding a balance of, okay, how much can I say and how much is just blatantly disrespectful? Like how far can I push my criticism, so it still feels constructive and not like the teacher feels attacked? It kind of goes for the same for speaking up when it comes to friends' parents because they are still authority figures.

And that's where I think things can get weird with parenting because some parents view it as 'I am above you.' I am in charge of all of your actions. And then I think they sometimes want to try and control their child's emotions and decisions.

If a parent was watching this and thinking, okay, I'm not going to use punishments, or I'm going to stop yelling at my kids or stop threatening them. What advice would you give them? Or maybe words of wisdom.

There's a very strong line between stopping yelling and stopping punishment and shutting down and not communicating because then the parent will start to resent whatever the kid is doing because they're like, 'oh well, now I can't yell at, and I can't punish them. So I have no other means of getting my point across.'

So it's a learning curve of no, you still do have to communicate all of your emotions, but the same way you would in any other relationship in your life. It's not different. It's just letting go of being the authority figure and viewing it as a normal relationship with a person. Hurt goes both ways. Communication goes both ways. You can still be upset.

Like when you get stressed about work or whatever, if something else is going on, you'll say, oh, I'm really stressed about work right now. So then, if you're more short-tempered than usual, I think, oh, this isn't about me.

I was going to ask you one more thing. I mean, obviously, I've made mistakes with you. I'm not a perfect parent.

Mm-hmm.

What have you learned about forgiveness, or if you hurt somebody you love, have you learned anything about that?

When I get hurt, I like other people to back off and give me space. But my brother, for example, likes a lot of attention and physical closeness when he's hurt. Whereas I need space, they need to talk about it. I need to talk through things a lot, but I also need to take a lot of time to think about what I want to say.

So it's kind of a long process for me because I need time to cool down and then time to think.

So what I hear there is it's helpful for parents to understand how their child processes.

That is a big thing. How does your kid want to be treated when you upset them? How do you want to be treated when they upset you? Not just like, oh, you're disappointed in them. Because it is different for different people, because in this kind of communication-based relationship, there will be times when feelings get hurt, you know?

And I think sometimes parents think, if our children hurt our feelings, we can't talk about that, or we need to keep it to ourselves.

You just have to start communicating with your words instead of your actions.

RESOURCES

If you are interested in the work we do at the Jai Institute for Parenting, visit our website: https://www.jaiinstituteforparenting.com/

Parent coaching is the most fulfilling work on the planet (yes, we are biased).

You can also find a global directory of our Certified Parent Coaches if you'd like support in making the changes we share in this book.

You can find a directory of our coaches at https://coaches.jaiinstitute-forparenting.com/

To the parents doing the work of breaking generational patterns of control, wounding and trauma, thank you. We are so grateful for your commitment to a peaceful revolution of your very own.

ABOUT THE AUTHOR AND OUR CONTRIBUTORS

**Kiva Schuler,
Founder & CEO of The Jai Institute
for Parenting**

Kiva's passion for parenting stemmed from her own childhood experiences of neglect and trauma. Like many of her generation, she had a front-row seat to witness what she did not want for her children. In many ways, Jai is the fulfillment of a promise that she made to herself when she was 16 years old... that when she had children of her own, she would learn to parent them with compassion, consistency, and communication.

Kiva is a serial entrepreneur and has been the marketer behind many transformational brands. Passionate about bringing authenticity and integrity to marketing and sales, she's a sought-after mentor, speaker, and coach.

**Rebecca Lyddon,
Director of Education at The Jai Institute
for Parenting**

Rebecca is propelled by a vision whereby she sees children being cared for by adults who are wise, healthy, free, creative, strong, brave, and bold. As a Social Worker, Waldorf Educator, Astrologer, 5Rhythms dance practice, Playback Theater, and lifelong child advocate, Rebecca is thrilled to integrate all her skills as a certified Parent Coach and Group Trainer.

When Rebecca is not engrossed in deep soul work, she is laughing, dancing, singing, and celebrating her life with her beloved and their two children in Lawrence, Kansas.

Richard Dixson

Richard is the founder of Drama-Free Parenting, where he helps traumatized families create peaceful homes.

As a grandfather along with his wife, raising their four grandchildren has many joys and many challenges. Richard appreciates the value of helping parents develop healthy parenting behaviors that create safe and nurturing home environments for their children.

An advocate for adoptive and foster parents in Kansas and Missouri, Richard is a certified trauma-informed care parent coach, sought out by schools, daycare centers, nonprofit organizations, and other professional organizations to design customized trauma-informed care training using a new parenting method called 3C+.

Richard enjoys writing children's books based on Sophie the Unicorn character, who loves helping children with their life challenges. He believes that healed parents will parent differently and that all parents deserve a peaceful home.

Chris Irvine

Chris Irvine loves kids. She also loves parents. And she gets it. She gets how stressful it is to be a young person, how vital it is for kids to have strong connections with their parents, and how knowing that and making it happen are two very different things. Her work with parents helps them bridge that gap, so they can build the strong foundations necessary for kids to thrive in an increasingly complex and scary world.

Chris raised her two often mystifying children, an autistic daughter, and a neurotypical son with his own challenges. When she realized the old ways of parenting, even those prescribed by professionals, were failing spectacularly, she radically changed her approach, and her family was completely transformed. Now a Jai-certified parenting coach, she works with parents to help them transform their own families.

Her mission in life is to help families blossom—just as hers has—so their kids can not only survive, but thrive.

Ashley Anjien-Kumar

Ashley suffered from a distorted self-image and low self-worth as a child. These landed her in the hospital twice in an attempt to take her own life. Statistics show increased awareness about the importance of children's emotional well-being. And yet, things aren't getting better.

Today, more than ever, kids need empowerment. And, parents get to be the conscious, confident, and empowered family leaders kids need. In order for that to happen, parents need support! The longer we wait, the more we risk the chance of unalterable life events. Ashley's vision is to help kids and parents become confident and resilient, celebrate their authentic truths and know their worth. Today she helps families create connected and cohesive family teams as a trauma-informed Certified Master Parent Coach and Certified Wisdom Coach for Kids.

Lina Lie

Lina Lie grew up in Singapore, where she was raised under a very different kind of parenting from what this book advocates for. A former aspiring corporate executive turned certified parent coach and educator, Lina's journey started out organically with the sole intention to better herself as a mother. She is now the founder of The Heartful Mama, and is deeply passionate about supporting parents in their own unique beautiful-and-messy-at-the-same-time parenting journey.

Lina desires to bring authentic harmony back into the home, where every family member is seen, heard and loved for who they are. She considers it her honor to journey with parents in their path towards building heartful connections within their families, keeping that spark of parental joy alive, no matter how old their children are. When she is not occupied reading something parenting-related, you can find Lina at the nearby park with her two young kids or traveling somewhere new with her family.

Lina is currently based in Austin, Texas. You can find her at her website: www.theheartfulmama.com. She is also active on social media and you can connect with her on her Instagram handle @theheartfulmama-coach or on her Facebook Page @theheartfulmama.

Allyn Miller

After years of working with families as an early childhood teacher, Allyn became a certified parenting coach and founder of Child Connection. As the creator of the Pause~Presence~Play method, she helps exhausted moms survive and thrive through every tantrum and meltdown inside her Parenting 101 program. She also shares her parenting philosophy and insights as a blog contributor for the Jai Institute for Parenting and The Baby Chick.

When not celebrating "aha" moments with her clients, you can find this chocoholic mama splashing in the ocean waves near her home of Weston, Florida or snuggled on the couch with her husband and two kids watching the latest Pixar movie.

Daisy Umenyiora

Daisy (Adaeze Ajegwu), is a specialized parenting expert, motivational speaker, and child educator with a decade of demonstrable experience in contemporary parenting, child training, and education.

Daisy is a Doctor of Philosophy (PhD) candidate at the University of Abuja, Nigeria. She holds a B.A. in English Language and a Masters in Curriculum Studies. She has professional certifications in Emotional Intelligence, Early Childhood Education, Child Psychology, and an honor-code Edx Certificate in Child Rights and Protection from the prestigious Harvard University, Cambridge, USA. She is a certified parenting coach with the renowned Jai Institute of Parenting.

Daisy demonstrates great enthusiasm and passion for the development of the female child. She affirms the application of philosophical principles and proffers psychological-based techniques in parent-child relationship management.

Jenny Warner

Jenny is a mom, a wife, and a lover of life. She is a Holistic Family Advisor, along with being a certified Life & Parent Coach, who truly loves to share information with parents so they can make deep connections in their life and transform their families. Jenny helps parents discover new ways to connect as a family on a whole new level. This level of connection revolutionizes families to become more aware, confident, resilient, and happy humans. Parents discover new ways to feel confident & loosen their grip a little so their children can really blossom.

Providing a safe space for parents to collaborate and figure out what works best for their family brings joy to so many families and that is what we do at I Shine Brite.com. Jenny's wish is to help you find peace so that you feel empowered in your parenting and can experience wonder and joy daily.

Thank you to these additional contributors:

Katie Owen, Isha McCaskey, Pam Snyder, Michelle Landau, Sara Janjigian-Trifiro and Destini Davis